DIVIDE AND RULE

State-Sponsored Ethnic Violence in Kenya

Africa Watch

Human Rights Watch
New York • Washington • Los Angeles • London

ISBN 1-56432-117-7
LCCCN: 93-80909

HUMAN RIGHTS WATCH

Human Rights Watch conducts regular, systematic investigations of human rights abuses in some sixty countries around the world. It addresses the human rights practices of governments of all political stripes, of all geopolitical alignments, and of all ethnic and religious persuasions. In internal wars it documents violations by both governments and rebel groups. Human Rights Watch defends freedom of thought and expression, due process of law and equal protection of the law; it documents and denounces murders, disappearances, torture, arbitrary imprisonment, exile, censorship and other abuses of internationally recognized human rights.

Human Rights Watch began in 1978 with the founding of Helsinki Watch by a group of publishers, lawyers and other activists and now maintains offices in New York, Washington, D.C., Los Angeles, London, Moscow, Belgrade, Bucharest and Hong Kong. Today, it includes Africa Watch, Americas Watch, Asia Watch, Helsinki Watch, Middle East Watch, and four collaborative projects, the Arms Project, Prison Project, Women's Rights Project, and the Fund for Free Expression. Human Rights Watch is an independent, nongovernmental organization, supported by contributions from private individuals and foundations. It accepts no government funds, directly or indirectly.

The executive committee includes Robert L. Bernstein, chair; Adrian W. DeWind, vice chair; Roland Algrant, Lisa Anderson, Peter D. Bell, Alice L. Brown, William Carmichael, Dorothy Cullman, Irene Diamond, Jonathan Fanton, Alan Finberg, Jack Greenberg, Alice H. Henkin, Stephen L. Kass, Marina Pinto Kaufman, Alexander MacGregor, Peter Osnos, Bruce Rabb, Orville Schell, Gary Sick, and Malcolm Smith.

The staff includes Kenneth Roth, executive director; Holly J. Burkhalter, Washington director; Gara LaMarche, associate director; Ellen Lutz, California director; Susan Osnos, press director; Jemera Rone, counsel; Michal Longfelder, Development director; Stephanie Steele, operations director; Allyson Collins, research associate; Joanna Weschler, Prison Project director; Kenneth Anderson, Arms Project director; Dorothy Q. Thomas, Women's Rights Project director; and Gara LaMarche, the Fund for Free Expression director.

The executive directors of the divisions of Human Rights Watch are Abdullahi An-Na'im, Africa Watch; Juan E. Méndez, Americas Watch; Sidney Jones, Asia Watch; Jeri Laber, Helsinki Watch; and Andrew Whitley, Middle East Watch.

Addresses for Human Rights Watch

485 Fifth Avenue
New York, NY 10017-6104
Tel: (212) 972-8400
Fax: (212) 972-0905
email: hrwatchnyu@igc.org

10951 West Pico Blvd., #203
Los Angeles, CA 90064
Tel: (310) 475-3070
Fax: (310) 475-5613
email: hrwatchla@igc.org

1522 K Street, N.W., #910
Washington, DC 20005
Tel: (202) 371-6592
Fax: (202) 371-0124
email: hrwatchdc@igc.org

90 Borough High Street
London, UK SE1 1LL
Tel: (071) 378-8008
Fax: (071) 378-8029
email: africawatch@gn.org

Districts in Kenya's Rift Valley, Western and Nyanza Provinces

CONTENTS

EFFECTS OF THE VIOLENCE

ACRONYMS

APP	African People's Party
CID	Criminal Investigations Department
DC	District Commissioner
DO	District Officer
DP	Democratic Party
FAO	Food and Agriculture Organization
FORD	Forum for the Restoration of Democracy
FORD-A	Forum for the Restoration of Democracy-Asili
FORD-K	Forum for the Restoration of Democracy-Kenya
GEMA	Kikuyu, Embu and Meru Cultural Association
GSU	General Service Unit
ICJ	International Commission of Jurists
KADU	Kenya African Democratic Union
KANU	Kenya African National Union
KDU	Kenya Democratic Union
Kshs.	Kenya Shillings (exchange rate of US$1 = Kshs.80 in this report)
LSK	Law Society of Kenya
MP	Member of Parliament
NCCK	National Council of Churches of Kenya
NDEHURIO	National Democratic Human Rights Organization
NEMU	National Election Monitoring Unit
PC	Provincial Commissioner
PCEA	Presbyterian Church of East Africa
UNDP	United Nations Development Program
UNHCR	United Nations High Commissioner for Refugees

PREFACE

This report is based on a visit to Kenya from June 17 to July 18, 1993, by an Africa Watch delegation consisting of Binaifer Nowrojee, a consultant to Africa Watch, and Africa Watch Orville Schell Fellow Bronwen Manby. In Kenya, the delegation travelled to seven of the districts that have been most affected by the ethnic clashes: Kericho, Nakuru, Bungoma, Trans Nzoia, Uasin Gishu, Nandi, and Kisumu. The delegation interviewed approximately 200 victims of the violence, many at the camps and market centers to which they have fled. In each area, the delegation interviewed Kalenjin and non-Kalenjin victims.

On June 29, 1993, in Uasin Gishu District, the delegation was prevented from speaking with clash victims at Laingushe camp in the Burnt Forest area by plainclothes reserve police and the assistant sub-chief of the area. The reason given was that speaking with the victims might incite violence. The officials involved refused to disclose their names, although they noted those of the Africa Watch delegation.

In Nairobi, the delegation met with a wide range of Kenyans, including lawyers, human rights activists, journalists, doctors, clergy, local government authorities, and Members of Parliament from all political parties, including the ruling Kenya African National Union (KANU). A meeting was also held with Attorney-General Amos Wako. A request for a meeting with officials in the Office of the President received no response.

Based on the mission and subsequent research, this report examines the Kenyan government's role in instigating and exacerbating "ethnic" violence for political gain. It also examines the government's failure to act to end the violence as well as its harassment and intimidation of those who attempt to end it.

The report was written by Binaifer Nowrojee and edited by Bronwen Manby and Africa Watch Executive Director Abdullahi An-Na'im. We express our gratitude to all the individuals and organizations who assisted us in the preparation of the report.

1. INTRODUCTION

President Daniel arap Moi of Kenya confidently predicted that the return of his country to a multiparty system would result in an outbreak of tribal violence that would destroy the nation. His prediction has been alarmingly fulfilled. One of the most disturbing developments in Kenya over the last two years has been the eruption of violent clashes between different ethnic groups. However, far from being the spontaneous result of a return to political pluralism, there is clear evidence that the government was involved in provoking this ethnic violence for political purposes and has taken no adequate steps to prevent it from spiralling out of control. So far, Africa Watch estimates that the clashes have left at least 1,500 people dead and 300,000 displaced. If action is not swiftly taken, there is a real danger that Kenya could descend into civil war.

In late 1991, concerted domestic and international pressure on the Moi government, including the suspension of aid by the World Bank and bilateral donors pending economic and human rights reforms, forced it to repeal a 1982 amendment to the constitution and legalize a multiparty system. One year later, in December 1992, elections finally took place. President Moi and the ruling party, the Kenya African National Union (KANU), were returned to power. Although Moi's reelection owed much to divisions among the opposition parties, the election campaign was also marred by significant irregularities.

Most seriously, the return to multipartyism coincided with the eruption of ethnic violence in Kenya's Rift Valley, Nyanza, and Western Provinces. This area, known as the "White Highlands" during British colonial rule, is Kenya's most fertile farmland. At first portrayed by the government as the result of long-standing conflict over land, or the spontaneous response of ethnically divided communities to the heated election campaign, these "tribal clashes" pitted members of Moi's own ethnic group, the Kalenjin, against the Kikuyu, Luhya, and Luo communities. However, it soon became clear that the violence was being coordinated. In September 1992, a parliamentary committee, formed only of KANU members, confirmed reports that high-ranking government officials had been involved in training and arming "Kalenjin

1

warriors," as they came to be known, to attack villages and drive away those from other ethnic groups.

It was hoped that the clashes would cease after President Moi was reelected in December 1992. However, that has not proved to be the case. Violence continued in 1993, returning with particular force towards the end of the year.

The reports of the attacks are remarkably similar. Hundreds of young men, dressed in an informal uniform of shorts and tee-shirts, armed with traditional bows and arrows, attack farms inhabited by Kikuyus, Luhyas, or Luos, all communities associated with the political opposition.   The warriors loot, kill, and burn, leaving death and destruction in their wake. To a lesser extent, there have been retaliatory attacks against the Kalenjin, though these have been less organized and more opportunistic in character, creating an escalating cycle of violence. There is a growing atmosphere of hatred and suspicion between communities that had lived together peacefully for many years.

Once an area is affected by violence, the inhabitants' lives are indefinitely disrupted. Continuing attacks prevent a return to the land. Living in squalid, unhygienic camps, without proper sanitation or shelter from the rain, these formerly productive citizens have become refugees in their own country. Many of those kept off their land report that it has been illegally occupied by the attackers, or that they have been offered sums significantly below market value for its purchase.   Where the displaced have managed to return to their land, they have lost all their belongings and are destitute, having missed a planting season.

The government's response to the violence has been characterized by inaction towards the attackers and outright hostility against those who have sought to help the victims.   In many cases, refugees from the violence report that members of the police force and army stood by and did nothing while an attack took place.   Police and judicial authorities have proved reluctant to arrest and sanction the majority of the attackers. Local government officials have on occasion forcibly dispersed refugee camps, while harassing church officers and others attempting to provide relief.   Although the govenment in Nairobi has claimed that its has distributed KSh.10 million ($125,000) of relief, little of this has reached the victims.

Furthermore, the violence has coincided with calls by high-ranking Kalenjins within the government for the creation of a *majimbo* system of government in Kenya, a federal system based on ethnicity. The proponents of *majimboism* have simultaneously called for the expulsion of all other ethnic groups from land occupied before the colonial era by the Kalenjin and other pastoral groups, including the Maasai, Turkana, and Samburu. Inflammatory statements by these figures have been ignored by the government, while similar calls made by opposition politicians have led to immediate action, including arrest and detention.

In September 1993, the government finally responded when renewed violence broke out in the Molo area of Nakuru District in the southwest of Rift Valley Province. Three areas, including Molo, were declared "security operation zones" and sealed off by security personnel, prohibiting individuals from outside the area to enter. The legality of these declarations is currently being challenged by human rights lawyers.

These recent actions by the government, two years after the violence began, appear to be designed to deflect international and domestic criticism without resolving the crisis. The government's actions come shortly before deliberations by international donors on November 22, 1993, on whether to resume the foreign aid being withheld on human rights grounds. The government has been quick to assert that it has ended the clashes. However, in the meantime, the violence has flared up elsewhere in Rift Valley Province.

Although the violence is portrayed by the government as purely ethnic or "tribal," its basis is clearly political. The Moi government and much of his Kalenjin community have stood to benefit economically and politically from the violence, even after the election. The polarized ethnic sentiments guarantee continued Kalenjin support for KANU. Moreover, the violence has been used to reward and empower the Kalenjin community by allowing its members to occupy land previously held by other groups in the fertile Rift Valley Province. At the same time, the violence has served to destabilize areas from which the political opposition would have been able to garner considerable political support, and to punish ethnic groups that have supported the political opposition. The gradual transformation of the Rift Valley Province into a Kalenjin land-owning area, as non-Kalenjins abandon or sell their farms, also has significant political implications. Since the Rift Valley Province is allocated the largest number of seats in Parliament, the KANU government is making long-term political gains in a future election by consolidating Kalenjin political hegemony.

The ultimate responsibility for ending the violence lies with President Moi. The implications of this incitement of ethnic rivalries for partisan political gain are deeply disturbing. If the government does not provide a lasting political solution for reconciliation and resettlement soon, the prospect of escalating violence and indiscriminate reprisals against the Kalenjin community appears likely. The culture of violence that is taking root has made real the alarming possibility of civil war in Kenya, for which the government will bear a significant measure of responsibility.

2. BACKGROUND

ETHNICITY AND POLITICS IN POST-INDEPENDENCE KENYA

Kenya is made up of over forty different ethnic groups ranging in size from a few hundred to more than a million members. The three largest are the Kikuyu, at twenty-one percent of the population; the Luhya[1], at approximately fourteen percent; and the Luo at approximately thirteen percent. Other smaller ethnic groups and their approximate percentages include the Kamba, eleven percent; the Kalenjin,[2] eleven percent; the Kisii, six percent; the Meru, five and a half percent; the Maasai, one and a half percent; the Turkana, one and a half percent and the Teso, one percent.[3] There are also small Indian, Arab, and European immigrant communities who are Kenyan nationals.

When Kenya became independent in 1963, the constitution set up a multi-party system, which allowed three leading political parties to contest the pre-independence general elections of 1963--the Kenya

---

[1] The Luhya consist of sixteen groups: Bukusu, Dakho, Kabras, Khayo, Kisa, Marachi, Maragoli, Marama, Nyala, Nyole, Samia, Tachoni, Tiriki, Tsotso, and Wanga. Like Kalenjin, the term Luhya is a creation of the colonial period.

[2] The Kalenjin actually consist of a number of distinct Nilotic ethnic groups that share similar linguistic and cultural traditions--the Kipsigis, Nandi, Pokot (or Suk), Elgeyo, Marakwet, Keiyo, Tugen, Sabaot, Sebei, Dorobo, and Terik. In pre-colonial times, the various Kalenjin groups had few political links. During the colonial period, they were officially referred to by the British colonial administration as Nandi-speaking or Mnandi. Most Kalenjin are semi-nomadic pastoralists and traditionally did not practice agriculture. The term Kalenjin, which was first used in the late 1950s, means "I tell you" in all the Kalenjin languages. The choice of the word was guided by the need to find one word common among all the groups. See B.E. Kipkorir, *People of the Rift Valley*, Kenya's People series, Evans Brothers, Nigeria (1978).

[3] These figures, while outdated, are based on the last official government census of 1979. Kenya, Ministry of Economic Planning and Development, Central Bureau of Statistics, *Statistical Abstract, 1981*, Nairobi (1981), p. 14, as reported in *Kenya: A Country Study*, American University Foreign Areas Studies, Washington DC (1984), p. 91.

5

National African Union (KANU), the Kenya African Democratic Union (KADU) and the African People's Party (APP). KANU, under Jomo Kenyatta, Oginga Odinga and Tom Mboya, was dominated by the country's two largest ethnic groups, the Kikuyu and Luo. The smaller ethnic groups, who had been marginalized in the independence negotiations as well as alienated from their land by the colonial settlers, sought to counter this perceived ethnic domination by forming KADU.

From its inception, KADU pursued a political philosophy of federalism, called *majimboism* (meaning regionalism in Kiswahili), which would allow semi-autonomous regions, based on ethnicity, to have substantial decision-making power. The central government would, in turn, have a limited and defined federal role. A coalition of the smaller ethnic groups, including the Kalenjin, led by Masinde Muliro, Daniel arap Moi, and Ronald Ngala, were strong proponents of *majimboism*, arguing that it would ensure that no single large ethnic group could dominate the country. KADU received significant funding from the British settler population before independence to counter support for KANU, which was identified with strong nationalist sentiment. However, with KANU's victory in the election, *majimboism* was quickly abandoned. Soon after, Kenya became a *de facto* one party state, following the voluntary dissolution of KADU and the APP. The political system was replaced with a strong, centralized KANU government, and regional powers were abolished.[4]

KANU rule under Kenya's first president, Jomo Kenyatta, was characterized by strong Kikuyu nationalist sentiments. In 1969, President Kenyatta banned attempts by Luo opposition leader Oginga Odinga to form a second political party in 1969. The move was seen by many Kenyans not only as a means of ensuring the preeminence of KANU, but also that of the Kikuyu. Although President Kenyatta was always careful to maintain a semblance of national (ethnically based) representation, including a Kalenjin vice-president (Moi himself), the government nonetheless was led by an inner circle of Kikuyu that promoted Kikuyu interests. Some members of this Kikuyu elite were connected to the Gikuyu [Kikuyu], Embu, Meru Association (GEMA), a tribal organization dedicated to keeping political power in Kikuyu hands. Prior to Kenyatta's

---

[4] Colin Leys, *Underdevelopment in Kenya*, Heinemann London Ltd. (1975), p. 212 and *Kenya: A Country Study*, American University Foreign Areas Studies, Washington DC (1984), p. 28.

death, GEMA unsuccessfully attempted to introduce a constitutional amendment to perpetuate Kikuyu hegemony and to ensure that then Vice-President Moi would not succeed Kenyatta. Upon taking office, President Moi disbanded all ethnic associations, including GEMA.

President Moi's leadership style followed the flawed legacy he inherited in 1978 after the death of President Kenyatta. The legacy was characterized by political patronage, political killings and detentions, and restrictions on freedom of speech and association. When President Moi assumed the presidency, he announced that his leadership would follow the footsteps, *Nyayo*, of President Kenyatta. As Kenyatta had used a Kikuyu power base to promote disproportional privileges to the Kikuyu community, so Moi did for his community, the Kalenjin. KANU soon became a vehicle to promote Kalenjin political sentiments. By 1990, most senior positions in government, the military, security agencies, and state-owned corporations were held by Kalenjins. One of President Moi's best known speeches exhorted Kenyans to exhibit the same blind loyalty to him that he had displayed to Kenyatta:

> I call on all Ministers, Assistant Ministers and every other person to sing like parrots. During Mzee [a Kiswahili term of respect] Kenyatta's period I persistently sang the Kenyatta tune until people said "This fellow has nothing except to sing for Kenyatta." I say: I didn't have any ideas of my own. Why was I to have my own ideas? I was in Kenyatta's shoes and therefore, I had to sing whatever Kenyatta wanted. If I had sung another song, do you think Kenyatta would have left me alone? Therefore, you ought to sing the song I sing. If I put a full stop, you should also put a full stop.[5]

However, President Moi responded to political dissent with a severity that surprised even those Kenyans who had been critical of President Kenyatta's policies. While President Kenyatta had tolerated a degree of free expression and association, his successor considered any dissent tantamount to treason. Under President Moi, the level of human rights abuses, economic corruption, and political patronage rose sharply.

---

[5] Sept. 13, 1984, on President Moi's return from Addis Ababa as reported in Africa Watch, *Taking Liberties* (July 1991), p. 27.

Following a failed coup attempt in 1982, the Moi regime intensified efforts to consolidate power. Among other steps, the constitution was amended to make KANU the sole political party by law. The human rights situation deteriorated steadily, accompanied by decreased accountability for government actions. Government critics were jailed, often under the Preservation of Public Security Act, which permits indefinite detention without trial. Allegations of torture by police authorities were widespread. Politically motivated charges were brought regularly against perceived government opponents.[6] Increasing political discontent and economic decline fueled a growing resentment of the political benefits given by President Moi to the Kalenjin.

Domestic pressure for political liberalization grew in response to the increasing repression. President Moi resisted calls for a multi-party system, threatening that the country would disintegrate into tribal violence.[7] The Law Society of Kenya (LSK) and the church led the renewed demands on President Moi to end the one-party state. Multi-party advocates called for a rally at Kamakunji, Nairobi, on July 7, 1990, which was attended by thousands of supporters. The rally was brutally dispersed by police and security forces, sparking off three days of rioting, known as the *Saba Saba* riots.[8] In August 1991, a coalition group called the Forum for the Restoration of Democracy (FORD) was created to call for greater political pluralism. Politically motivated charges were immediately brought against prominent FORD members.

Increasing discontent with the government's lack of accountability eventually prompted Kenya's international donors to join the domestic calls for change by suspending all foreign aid. In November 1991, a joint meeting of donor nations and the World Bank issued an ultimatum to the government suspending over $1 billion a year in foreign aid until the government instituted political and economic reforms. One month later, the Kenyan Parliament repealed Section 2(a) of the Constitution, which had legitimized one-partyism in Kenya.[9]

---

[6] See Africa Watch, *Taking Liberties* (July 1991).

[7] "Moi Warns of Tribal Conflict," *Daily Telegraph*, December 31, 1991.

[8] *Saba Saba* means "seven seven" (July 7) in Kiswahili.

[9] See "Democracy in Kenya?" *Reconstruction*, Vol. 2, No. 1 (1992), p. 52.

THE ELECTION

On December 29, 1992, a year after a multi-party system was legalized, Kenya held its first genuine multi-party elections since independence. President Moi was reelected with just over 36 percent of the vote, and KANU returned as the largest party in the National Assembly. The reelection of President Moi and KANU, both undoubtedly unpopular after their many years in power, owed much to divisions and in-fighting within the three major opposition parties, the Forum for the Restoration of Democracy-Kenya (FORD-K); the Forum for the Restoration of Democracy-Asili (FORD-A); and the Democratic Party (DP). FORD-A and FORD-K were splinter groups of the original FORD coalition.[10]

International election observers criticized the process leading up to the election. The Commonwealth observer team noted significant irregularities including "widespread tribal disturbances, threats, and harassment of party supporters, in particular supporters of the opposition parties."[11] The team also noted a number of other problems that had undermined the electoral process, including a flawed registration process in many parts of the country; an unfair nominations process, particularly in the Rift Valley where sixteen KANU Parliamentary candidates ran unopposed; a lack of transparency on the part of the Electoral Commission; intimidation, administrative obstacles and violence that

---

[10] In the presidential race, President Moi won 1,964,421 votes (36 percent); Kenneth Matiba of FORD-A won 1,412,476 votes (26.21 percent); Mwai Kibaki of DP won 1,028,152 (19.08 percent); and Jaramogi Oginga Odinga of FORD-K won 944,197 (17.56 percent). In Parliament, KANU won one hundred seats; FORD-A and FORD-K won thirty-one each; DP won twenty-three; and three seats were won by small independent parties, for a total of 188 elected seats. Another twelve Members of Parliament are nominated by the President. *Standard*, January 5, 1992.

[11] Commonwealth Secretariat, *The Presidential, Parliamentary and Civic Elections in Kenya*, The Report of the Commonwealth Observer Group, December 29, 1992, p.(x).

marked political campaigns; partisanship of the state-owned media; and the reluctance of the government to de-link itself from KANU.[12]

In spite of these serious impediments, the observer team concluded its report by noting that "[d]espite the fact that the whole electoral process cannot be given an unqualified rating as free and fair, the evolution of the process to polling day and the subsequent count was increasingly positive to a degree that we believe that the results in many instances directly reflect, however imperfectly, the will of the people."[13]

A few months later, in April 1993, the World Bank released US$85 million in quick disbursal aid, citing economic reforms. The release of the aid came shortly after two major currency devaluations, a skyrocketing rate of inflation, and the exposure of a major government corruption scandal. However, the remainder--and bulk--of Kenya's foreign aid remains withheld pending further human rights and economic reforms.

MULTI-PARTY KENYA: A GROWING CULTURE OF VIOLENCE

Almost one year after the election victory by President Moi and KANU, the government's actions have indicated a continuation of the same style of leadership, characterized by repression and a lack of accountability. Although the political system was opened up to some extent by the elections, the government has remained intolerant of criticism. Attacks on opposition politicians and journalists, use of excessive force by police in the control of demonstrations, and the enforcement of repressive legislation remain serious human rights concerns. Members of the Kalenjin group continue to be promoted regardless of merit and to the exclusion of other ethnicities.[14]

---

[12] Ibid., p. 39.

[13] Ibid., p. 40.

[14] President Moi's new cabinet is dominated by members of his own Kalenjin group and that of Vice-President George Saitoti's Maasai. The Kikuyu and Luo have been given one representative each in the twenty-five member cabinet. In the local government administration, Kalenjin District Commissioners constitute the largest number from any ethnic group at fourteen out of sixty-seven. Among the district officers, seventy-six out of 489 are Kalenjin with the third largest

President Moi and his associates have not ceased their abuse of power, but merely have modified their tactics. Prior to the election, the Moi government had maintained power by directly attacking critics through blatant manipulation of the legislative and judicial systems. In response to domestic resistance and the conditioning of foreign aid to human rights, the Kenyan government has taken some steps to address these criticisms of its human rights record in the hope of securing the restoration of its foreign aid.[15]

Recently, the government has relied on different tactics, such as extra-legal intimidation and violence, to silence and disempower critics. The change in tactics appears to be a deliberate move on the part of the government to avoid international censure. A growing culture of state-sponsored harassment and vigilante violence against opposition leaders and other critics is being encouraged and fostered by the government. The chilling aspect of the violence is that the government usually denies any knowledge of or responsibility to it, attributing it instead to unknown vigilantes.[16]

---

number following the Kikuyu and Luo communities which are each represented by eighty-one. "Minister Gives Number of DCs," *Daily Nation*, June 24, 1993.

[15] In addition to the introduction of a multi-party system, prominent political prisoners were released unconditionally in 1992 and early 1993. The government stopped its practice of holding critics in indefinite detention without trial, pursuant to the Preservation of Public Security Act. In April 1993, a new chief justice, Fred Apaloo, replaced former Chief Justice Alan Hancox, a British expatriate, commonly accused of the erosion of judicial independence during his tenure. The government returned the confiscated passports of government critics and ratified the African Charter on Human and People's Rights.

[16]On occasion, the government's role in this violence is exposed. In March 1993, a group of Maasais dressed in traditional costume attacked opposition supporters at the state opening of Parliament. Maasai MP William ole Ntimama held a press conference, stating that the Maasais had acted in self defense. A month later, KANU Secretary-General Joseph Kamotho publicly admitted that the Maasai were part of a 3,000-strong youth squad hired by KANU for the occasion to "deal with the opposition supporters." Mr. Kamotho later denied the reports, despite the fact that he had verified the statement to an editor who had called him before publication. "A Convoluted Affair," *Weekly Review*, April 9, 1993, and "Morans: Speaker Wants Kamotho to Explain," *Daily Nation*, April 2, 1993.

The "ethnic" violence appears to be a manifestation of the government's employment of new methods to maintain power. As in South Africa and Zaire, the Kenyan government, forced by a combination of internal and external pressures to lift some forms of repression and allow elections to be held, apparently has fomented "ethnic" violence to circumvent the rule of law and undermine the process of political liberalization. As the general secretary of the National Council of Churches of Kenya (NCCK), Samuel Kobia, told Africa Watch,

> it is not a coincidence that this is happening. Leaders are setting up the people against each other, making the people do the government's dirty work. And then at the end of the day, you can say that there are just ethnic clashes--no human rights violations.[17]

THE CALL FOR MAJIMBOISM--KENYA'S ETHNIC CLEANSING

> *We are saying that unless those clamouring for political pluralism stop, we must devise a protective mechanism by launching this movement.*
>   -- Joseph Misoi, KANU MP for Eldoret South

The introduction of a multi-party system has also been accompanied by calls from Kalenjin and Maasai politicians in KANU for the introduction of the *majimbo* system proposed at independence. A number of high profile political rallies, known as *majimbo* rallies, have been held by certain Kalenjin and Maasai politicians who have asserted that the Rift Valley, which is allocated the largest number of seats in Parliament (44 of 188), was traditionally Kalenjin/Maasai territory and that other ethnic groups living in the area should not be permitted to express differing political views in a multi-party system.

The calls for *majimboism* have taken on a decidedly ominous tone. Its proponents have called for *majimboism* as a means of undermining the recent political liberalization and as a way of demanding the expulsion of all ethnic groups from the Rift Valley except for those pastoralist groups--

---

[17] Interview with Samuel Kobia, General Secretary NCCK, Nairobi, June 21, 1993.

Kalenjins, Maasai, Turkana and Samburu--that were on the land before colonialism. If implemented, *majimboism* would mean the expulsion of millions of members of other ethnic groups who have settled there since the 1920s and who have legally purchased land since the 1950s. In addition, few of the proponents of *majimboism* have attempted to articulate the mechanism--federalism, semi-autonomous states or regional confederations--by which such a system could be established.

While many Kenyans have no quarrel with the concept of regionalism, *per se*, they view these calls as nothing less than calls for ethnic cleansing. Not coincidentally, the ethnic groups which these *majimboism* proponents are proposing should be expelled from the Rift Valley Province are predominantly the Kikuyu, Luhya, and Luo, who are perceived to support the political opposition.[18]

The most virulent proponents of this form of *majimboism* include Vice-President George Saitoti; MP Nicholas Biwott; Minister for Local Government William ole Ntimama, and MP for Eldoret South, Joseph Misoi. Mr. ole Ntimama, a Maasai, argues that with the introduction of a multi-party system, the survival of the smaller ethnic groups has been threatened and that *majimboism* is "the only way out to safeguard the interest of the smaller tribes and check the colonization and oppression experienced presently."[19] With increasing frequency, these and other Kalenjin and Maasai KANU politicians have referred to Kikuyus and others as "aliens" and "foreigners" in the Rift Valley as opposed to "natives" or "original inhabitants."[20] A month before the ethnic clashes began, in a seemingly coordinated move, top Kalenjin politicians arranged a series of political rallies in Rift Valley Province calling for *majimboism*.

At a rally held on September 8, 1991, in Kapsabet (Nandi District, Rift Valley Province), Kalenjin MP Joseph Misoi read a statement declaring that a *majimbo* constitution had been drafted that would be tabled before the House if proponents of a multi-party system continued

---

[18] See "*Majimboism*: Stirring for Blood Hatred," *Nairobi Weekly*, June 29, 1993, p. 13.

[19] See "Can *Majimboism* Work?" *Kenya Times*, May 20, 1993, p. 14, and "*Majimboism*: The Pros and Cons," *Kenya Times*, May 21, 1993, p. 12.

[20] "Indigenous or Native? How Ntimama Sees It," *Daily Nation*, June 30, 1993.

their efforts. At the meeting, it was also resolved that action would be taken against multi-party proponents; that they would fight using all means at their disposal to protect the government and the ruling party KANU; and that they would "ban" Paul Muite (multi-party advocate and then Chair of the Law Society of Kenya) from setting foot in Rift Valley Province. Under this constitution, "outsiders" in the Rift Valley Province would be required to go back to their "motherland."[21]

At a second rally held on September 21, 1991, in Kapkatet (Kericho District, Rift Valley Province), the Kalenjin politicians present resolved to "ban" multi-party advocates from setting foot in Rift Valley Province and ordered the late Musinde Muliro (a founding member of FORD) to move out of Rift Valley Province. They further condemned the Nairobi leaders for allowing multi-party advocates to remain in Nairobi and called for the proscription of the Law Society of Kenya, which had been at the forefront of the multiparty debate.

At the same rally, Kalenjin MP Nicholas Biwott, warned that FORD members would be "crushed" and that KANU youth wingers would be ready to fight to the last person to protect the Moi government.[22] He added that Kalenjins were not cowards and were ready to counter any attempt to remove them from leadership. Other politicians at the meeting called on Kalenjins to "crush" government critics and to report them to the police. Calls were also made at the meeting for Kalenjins to be ready to protect the government using any weapons at their disposal and to arm themselves with bows and arrows to destroy any multiparty

---

[21] The politicians present at the meeting included Chairman of KANU-Nandi branch Henry Kosgey; Ministers John Cheruiyot and Timothy Mibei; Assistant Ministers Kipkalia Kones, Eric Bomett, and Willy Kamuren; MPs Paul Chepkok, Benjamin Kositany, Ezekiel Barngetuny; and thirty-four councillors from Nandi, Kericho/Bomet, and Nakuru Districts.   Republic of Kenya, *Report of the Parliamentary Select Committee to investigate Ethnic Clashes in Western and Other Parts of Kenya* (Sept. 1992), p. 8-9. See also "Memories of 1991," *Weekly Review*, April 9, 1992, p. 9.

[22] President Moi created a youth wing within KANU, vesting it with police powers to look out for "anti-party elements." The KANU youthwingers are known for their indiscriminate violence, thuggery and extortion. Africa Watch, *Taking Liberties*, (July 1991), p. 14.

advocate in sight.[23]   These and other *majimbo* rallies held before the election are believed by many Kenyans to have contributed to ongoing ethnic antagonism.   Yet no KANU politicians responsible for such comments were publicly censured or held accountable by President Moi.

The *majimbo* rallies have continued since the election. At a rally in April 1993, William ole Ntimama, the Maasai Minister for Local Government and MP for Narok North, alleged that the political opposition was arming itself as a plot to eliminate indigenous residents of the Rift Valley. He told the "true" Rift Valley residents (the Kalenjin, Maasai, Samburu, and Turkana) to be on their guard and to spread the message so that they could defend themselves.   Vice-President George Saitoti, another Maasai, affirmed Mr. Ntimama's words, followed by a Minister of State in the Office of the President, Kipkalia Kones, a Kalenjin who declared that the Rift Valley Province would have only Kalenjin Members of Parliament.[24]

President Moi and his Kalenjin supporters have consistently portrayed the calls for political pluralism and a multi-party system as an anti-Kalenjin movement. Accordingly, President Moi and his inner circle have been able to mobilize the Kalenjin community on ethnic grounds as a means of consolidating their economic and political power base. The Maasai and the Turkana, traditionally pastoralist groups, have also been aligned with Kalenjin political aspirations.

As part of this ethnic mobilization, Kalenjin attackers responsible for the recent "ethnic" violence in Kenya have embraced traditional Kalenjin symbols. Kalenjin attackers have used traditional weapons-- bows and arrows--to attack other ethnic groups. Often, attackers' faces are painted with clay markings, characteristic of the markings used during the rite of initiation, a central feature of Kalenjin life. Initiation is always carried out after circumcision and is designed to prepare a youth

---

[23] The politicians present at this meeting were Ministers Timothy Mibei, Nicholas Biwott, and John Cheruiyot; Assistant Ministers Kipkalia Kones, Francis Mutwol, Willy Kamuren, William Kikwai, John Terer, Lawi Kiplagat, Christopher Lomada, and Peter Nangole; and MPs Ayub Chepkwony, Robert Kipkorir and Samson ole Tuya. Republic of Kenya, *Report of the Parliamentary Select Committee to investigate Ethnic Clashes in Western and Other Parts of Kenya* (Sept. 1992), p. 9-10.

[24] "Feeling the Heat?" *Weekly Review*, April 9, 1992, p. 3.

to be a full adult member of his society. As part of this initiation, young boys are taught to use bows and arrows. A Kalenjin told Africa Watch:

> Kalenjins have always had bows and arrows. The young men at circumcision are trained in the use of bows, not for killing, but as a matter of tradition; there are two types of arrows, poisoned and non-poisoned. If you are hit by a poisoned arrow anywhere on your body, you die. Because all Kalenjins are trained to use bows and arrows, it is easy for the Kalenjin to organize this way for fighting.[25]

Disturbingly, this type of sectarian mobilization is becoming increasingly common in Kenya. Kenya's Muslim population, prohibited from registering the Islamic Party of Kenya, has clashed several times with the police in riots protesting the government's action. In September 1993, a group of prominent Kikuyus called for the resurrection of the defunct ethnically based group, Gikuyu [Kikuyu], Embu and Meru Association (GEMA). Increasingly, the political debate in Kenya is becoming polarized on ethnic lines, even within the political opposition.

LAND OWNERSHIP IN THE RIFT VALLEY

The recent ethnic violence in Kenya has predominantly affected Kenya's most fertile farming area--the Rift Valley Province. Kenya is divided into eight Provinces: Rift Valley, Nyanza, Western, Central, Eastern, North Eastern, Nairobi, and Coast.[26] This area, covering forty percent of Kenya's land mass, formed the core of the so called "White Highlands" during British colonial rule. Prior to the colonial period, the area was the home of pastoral nomadic groups, including the Kalenjin, Maasai, Samburu, and Turkana peoples.

---

[25] Interview with Kalenjin man, Nakuru, Nakuru District, June 25, 1993.

[26] The provinces are administered through local government officials led by the provincial commissioner (PC). Each province is subdivided into districts and administered by a district commissioner (DC) and district officers (DO). All local government officials, including the local chiefs, are direct appointees of the President's Office.

British colonial rule in Kenya had a profound effect on land ownership and tenure in the Rift Valley area. It established relations between ethnic groups that previously had no significant interaction and permanently altered the ethnic composition of the population in the Rift Valley. A succession of land regulations between 1899 and 1915 expropriated much of the best land in the highlands from the area's inhabitants and reserved it for white settlers. The colonial administration instituted policies barring Africans from owning land in this area and restricting Africans to native reserves. Pastoralist groups that had enjoyed customary rights over the land found themselves excluded from areas they had used in the past. The creation of this white area, reserved for British settler occupation, dislocated and disinherited thousands of Africans who had lived in the Rift Valley.

Additionally, the colonial government introduced coercive measures to create a large, cheap African labor force to service the white settler farms.[27] The pastoralist population in the area, lacking farming experience, proved unsuitable for providing cheap agricultural labor to the settlers. To overcome the labor shortage, the colonial administration recruited labor from the neighboring areas (now Central, Nyanza and Western Provinces). Thousands of Kikuyu, Kisii, Luhya, and Luo squatters were brought into Rift Valley Province as sharecropper labor in the early 1900s.[28]

The issue of land alienation, coupled with increasing discontent with repressive British colonial rule, led to the rise of a nationalist movement for independence. In 1952, a state of emergency was declared by the British in response to the rise of an armed independence movement known as the Mau Mau, which was led predominantly by the Kikuyu squatter population. By 1961, the British were forced to make concessions, and a new policy in the White Highlands was introduced that allowed Africans to buy land and farm there.

At Kenya's independence in 1963, the land issue was never fully addressed. British settler interests were safeguarded, while no effort was

---

[27] These financial and political measures included the introduction of the Hut and Poll taxes, the Masters and Servants Ordinance and the Kipande (pass book) system to mention a few.

[28] Tabitha Kanogo, *Squatters and the Roots of Mau Mau, 1905-63*, Heinemann Kenya Ltd. (1987), p. 14.

made to deal with the competing claims of those pastoral ethnic groups who originally were ousted from the Rift Valley area by the British and subsequently the squatter labor who settled on the land. British settler farmers were given the option to retain the land they had expropriated through colonialism. Consequently, large tracts of the best farmland in Kenya remain in the ownership of British settlers. For those settlers that wanted to sell their land, a land settlement scheme was set up by the British and the newly independent Kenyan government to buy it. Kenyans, who had previously been squatter labor, were then able to buy land either individually or through collective schemes such as cooperatives, societies, and companies.

Among the Kikuyu, unlike communal pastoral groups such as the Maasai and Kalenjin, farming was an established practice. Accordingly, many Kikuyus were eager to take advantage of the opportunity to purchase land. Encouraged and assisted by President Kenyatta, large numbers of Kikuyu bought land in the Rift Valley during the 1960s and 1970s, and moved from the overcrowded Central Province. These farms have been at the center of the recent ethnic violence.

THE "ETHNIC" CLASHES

3. PRE-ELECTION VIOLENCE:
OCTOBER 1991--DECEMBER 1992

The ethnic clashes first broke out on October 29, 1991, at Meteitei farm in Tinderet, Nandi District, on the border of Rift Valley, Nyanza, and Western Provinces. At the time, political sentiments were running high, as domestic and international pressure for a multi-party system was mounting. The government portrayed the fighting as a simple land dispute. Initially, the explanation seemed convincing and people from the region drew the same conclusion likening the dispute to a similar incident between the Nandi and Luhya ethnic groups that had taken place in 1984 at Kapkangani.[29]

However, within days, the fighting had escalated, taking on an ethnic component. As the fighting continued, the Kalenjin community was accused of attacking the Luo community. Victims of the fighting reported that the attacks were politically motivated and that their attackers had vowed to drive non-Kalenjins and opponents of KANU from the Rift Valley Province. Luo leaders, whose community was the first to be affected by the clashes, concluded that the violence was the direct result of the *majimbo* rally held at Kapsabet a month earlier. After the violence erupted, leaflets were distributed in the area warning Luos and other non-Kalenjins to leave the area by December 12, 1991, or "face the consequences." The leaflets were signed by a group calling itself the Nandi Warriors.

Reports emerging from the clash areas were remarkably similar. In most cases, hundreds of Kalenjin "warriors," as they became known, would attack farms, targeting non-Kalenjin houses. The attackers were often identically dressed in an informal uniform of shorts and tee-shirts (sometimes red, sometimes black) and always armed with traditional bows and arrows as well as pangas (machetes). Sometimes, the warriors would have their faces marked in the traditional manner with clay. The warriors would loot, kill, and burn houses, leaving death and destruction in their wake.

---

[29] "A Story of Indelible Damage," *Weekly Review*, March 20, 1992, p. 10.

In November 1991, two Luo MPs, Onyango Midika and Miruka Owour, brought a motion in Parliament to discuss the clashes as an issue of national importance. However, they withdrew the motion the same day, after receiving assurances from the government that it would do all in its power to end the clashes. The same day, a minister in the Office of the President, Joseph Ngutu, told Parliament that the number of casualties from the fighting had reached three. Press reports at the time estimated the death toll at six to ten and the displaced at approximately 50,000.[30] Catholic Bishop Mwana a'Nzeki estimated that the violence had resulted in over 1,000 houses being burned in the Rift Valley Province and the equivalent of one year's food destroyed and animals killed or stolen.

Despite the government's assurances, the clashes continued to spread. The following week, they reached neighboring Kericho District. The Kericho-Kisumu road was temporarily closed as "Kalenjin warriors" (Nandis) armed with bows and arrows battled with Luos across the road. The confrontation between the two communities followed an attack by Kalenjins against hundreds of Luos residing in Nandi and Kericho Districts during which the Kalenjins had looted and burned Luo homes. The Luo community responded with a counter-attack. A Luo policeman trying to stop the fighting allegedly killed a Kalenjin, resulting in a new attack by the Kalenjins against neighboring Owiro farm, populated by Luos. Press reports put the number of deaths at five.[31]

In December 1991, Parliament repealed Section 2(a) of the Constitution making Kenya officially a multi-party state. By that time, the fighting had affected large sections of the Rift Valley, Western, and Nyanza border areas, with the main targets being other ethnic groups living in Kalenjin areas. Increasingly, Luhya, Kikuyu, and Kisii ethnic groups began to be affected. The fighting spread north to Trans Nzoia District, and non-Kalenjins were attacked there on December 27, 1991. In one attack at Endebess, Trans Nzoia District, five people were reported killed, several injured, and seventy houses burned. A Kikuyu

---

[30] Ibid., p. 11.

[31] *Daily Nation*, November 10, 1991, as reported in NCCK, *The Cursed Arrow: Organized Violence Against Democracy in Kenya*, April 1992, p. 25.

bar owner, Njenga Kaheni, was singled out and killed by Kalenjins (Sabaots).[32]

As the fighting continued to rage in Kericho and Kisumu Districts, the newly legalized political opposition was quick to blame the ethnic clashes on the KANU government's fear of losing the election. They charged the government with instigating the violence to destabilize and intimidate areas with opposition support. In Kisumu District, clashes began when groups of Kalenjin warriors staged unprovoked attacks on the homes of the Luo and other ethnic groups living in the border areas, looting and then burning property. Another incident of violence was sparked off by the harassment of a political opposition supporter by KANU followers.[33]

Violence continued to spread after the new year began. In January 1992, fighting continued in Nandi and Kakamega Districts. Non-Kalenjin teachers in Trans Nzoia District reported that Kalenjin youths had threatened to lynch them if they reported to work.[34]

By February 1992, the clashes had escalated dramatically. The repeated claims by the government that it had deployed sufficient security to the clash areas were offset, both by the continuing violence and by the government's failure to sanction inflammatory statements by Kalenjin politicians, which appeared to fuel the violence further. Press reports described the "scores of displaced men, women and children, their salvaged personal effects on their heads and shoulders, stream[ing] endlessly to makeshift shelters." In Kabose village in Nandi District, one attack displaced one hundred people and left twenty-six homes burned.[35]   During the height of the violence, in March 1992, Kalenjin Assistant Minister Kipkalia Kones, declared that Kericho District was a KANU zone and added that anyone who supported the political

---

[32] *Daily Nation*, December 27, 1991, and *Standard*, December 29, 1991 as reported in NCCK, *The Cursed Arrow*, p. 25.

[33] "New Spate of Violence," *Weekly Review*, March 13, 1992, p. 18.

[34] *Daily Nation*, January 20 and 24, 1992, as reported in NCCK, *The Cursed Arrow*, p. 25.

[35] *Daily Nation*, February 4 and March 7, 1992 as reported in NCCK, *The Cursed Arrow*, p. 25 and 6.

opposition would "live to regret it." He also stated that the Kalenjin youth in the area had declared war on the Luo community within the district in retaliation for a number of Kalenjins killed in earlier violence.[36] Violence returned to the place where the clashes had first broken out, wreaking havoc for the second time at Meteitei farm in Nandi District. Not satisfied with driving non-Kalenjins off their farms, the Kalenjin warriors attacked displaced families camping in Lakhome Market in Trans Nzoia District. In Chemichimi, Bungoma District, Kalenjins attacked the Luhya community. The unrelenting attacks against non-Kalenjins resulted in a number of retaliatory attacks against Kalenjins. In Kisumu, a mob predominantly made up of Luos stoned cars belonging to Kalenjins. Director of Forestry Crispus Nyaga, reported in March 1992 that the clashes had resulted in 30,000 hectares of forest being burned down.[37]

Fighting also broke out on the border of West Pokot and Trans Nzoia Districts (near the Uganda border). This is an area long known for cattle-rustling between the Kalenjin (Pokot) and the Luo, Luhya and Kisii. In March 1992, the Kalenjin community launched attacks on the other communities. "This violence was different," the local parish councillor told Africa Watch, "before, they [the Pokot Kalenjins] were only stealing cattle, but now they are also burning houses and killing people. They still steal everyone's cattle. But they only burn the houses of the Bukusu [Luhya]."[38] A Luhya victim from the area also confirmed that "burning of houses began in this area in March 1992. The Pokots [Kalenjins] attacked us. This is a new thing that has not happened before, although stock theft has always taken place."[39] Another disturbing aspect about the attacks in the West Pokot-Trans Nzoia area was the fact that the

---

[36] "New Spate of Violence," *Weekly Review*, March 13, 1992, p. 18.

[37] *Daily Nation*, March 11, 29 and 31, 1992 as reported in NCCK, *The Cursed Arrow*, April 1992, p. 25-26.

[38] Interview with Parish Councillor, Kolongolo, Trans Nzoia District, June 30, 1993.

[39] Interview with Luhya clash victim, Kolongolo, Trans Nzoia District, June 29, 1993.

Kalenjin warriors used guns smuggled from Uganda, in addition to bows and arrows.

Thousands of people continued to flee their homes to nearby market centers and church compounds in search of sanctuary from the violence. The Catholic church estimated that within six months approximately 100,000 people had been displaced by the clashes. In April 1992, new clashes erupted between the Kisii and the Maasai while fighting continued in Bungoma District between the Kalenjin and the Luhya. Press reports estimated that 2,000 people were displaced in Bungoma District alone. In one attack in Bungoma District on April 12, 1992, fourteen were killed, 120 houses burned and thirty-seven cattle were stolen.[40] In another attack at Chebiyuk, a witness told Africa Watch:

> The Sabaots [Kalenjin] attacked us in April 1992 after the clashes started in Trans Nzoia. They had bows and arrows and also guns and pangas. They were wearing tee-shirts and red shorts and red and white clay on their faces. As they attacked, they were shouting "madoadoa" which means "remove those spots." There were too many for us to know who they were and their faces were covered. They came from two directions at once. More than ten people were killed and others injured. As many as 2,000 houses were burned. No one was arrested in connection with this attack.[41]

Kalenjins increasingly became at risk of being victimized in retaliatory strikes as Luhyas, Luos and Kikuyus responded to the violence against them. In Kibigori, Kisumu District, Luos launched retaliatory attacks against Kalenjins. In nearby Chepsweta, Kalenjin homes were targeted by angry Luos on November 7, 1991. One young Kalenjin (Nandi) man told Africa Watch,

---

[40] *Daily Nation*, April 8, 9, 11, and 12, 1992, as reported in NCCK, *The Cursed Arrow*, April 1992, p. 28.

[41] Interview with Luhya clash victim, Kapkateny camp, Bungoma District, July 1, 1993.

My house was burned by a group of people shouting in
Luo. I and my family escaped and my house was burned
down. At first, I was too scared to come back, but now
it is alright [over two years later]. The main problem is
that people here are hungry. Most of them have had all
their belongings destroyed.[42]

Another old Kalenjin man who had lost all his belongings told Africa
Watch,

I came out of my house at around 11:00 P.M. and saw
burning houses and heard people screaming in Luo. I
saw people smashing things--maybe about 200 of them--I
shone a torch at them and recognized two of my
neighbors. They were wearing ordinary clothes, carrying
stones, slings, hammers, crow bars, and pangas. They
were shouting "Let's kill this old man." They broke into
my house and took everything including my cattle. I did
not report the attack to the police because I was afraid of
reprisals. I was not able to plant this past year so I have
no food.[43]

At Chepkube, Bungoma District, violence erupted in a Kalenjin
area in July 1992. The village was attacked one night by Luhyas wearing
black coats and caps, using guns, pangas, and spears.[44] By the time
they left, ten Kalenjins were dead. The assistant sub-chief, who is
Kalenjin, told Africa Watch that "although there were always inter-
community tensions and cattle rustling, this violence was different. This
violence was not connected to the regular violence which we have seen
in the past." When asked about the fact that many people perceive the

---

[42] Interview with Kalenjin (Nandi) clash victim, Chepsweta, Kisumu District,
July 2, 1993.

[43] Interview with old Kalenjin (Nandi) clash victim, Chepsweta, Kisumu
District, July 2, 1993.

[44] Interview with Kalenjin (Sabaot) clash victim, Chepkube, Bungoma District,
July 3, 1993.

violence to be instigated by the Kalenjin community he said, "I am Kalenjin. I have not gained from the government. My brother was killed in the clashes. I am a Chief for all, not just Kalenjins. Over 14,000 people were displaced by the violence. In this area, seventy percent are Kalenjin, twenty percent Bukusu [Luhya], and ten percent Teso."[45]

Simultaneously, fighting broke out in Olenguruone, Nakuru District. In 1939, the colonial government had settled over 4,000 Kikuyu squatters on the land, which had originally been part of Maasailand. Olenguruone was one of the most affected areas, and thousands of families fled the fighting--most of whom remain in temporary shelters to date. The fighting broke out when approximately 500 Kalenjins wearing black shorts and white shirts attacked the Kikuyus, Luhyas, and Kisiis in the area. The Kalenjin community from the area justified their actions to Africa Watch by saying that they were preempting an anticipated attack by the Kikuyu community.[46] The fighting continued for days as the Kikuyus grouped at Chepakundi and the Kalenjin (Kipsigis) at Korowa, approximately three kilometers away. According to a Kalenjin man who witnessed the fighting, the Kalenjin community used non-poisoned arrows at first and poisoned arrows later. He told Africa Watch,

> Both Kikuyus and Kalenjins torched each other's houses. By the time the fighting ended approximately twenty Kalenjins and 200 Kikuyus were dead. At Chepakundi, some Kikuyus surrendered. They were made to raise a fistful of grass in the air and say "KANU *juu*" [up with KANU].[47]

The government's response to the fighting in Olenguruone was to send forty extra policemen and a helicopter. However, this number was

---

[45] Interview with Kalenjin (Sabaot) assistant sub-chief, Chepkube, Bungoma District, July 3, 1993.

[46] Interview with Kalenjin (Kipsigis) men, Olenguruone, Nakuru District, June 25, 1993.

[47] Interview with Kalenjin (Kipsigis) man, Olenguruone, Nakuru District, June 25, 1993.

insufficient. Members of both communities who fled to the local district officer's offices for safety were told by the district officer to return to their homes, despite the fact that it was unsafe.[48]

On December 3, 1992, fighting broke out between Kalenjins and Kikuyus in the Burnt Forest area near Eldoret, Uasin Gishu District, resulting in approximately 15,000 people taking refuge at the Catholic church compound. Hundreds of Kalenjin warriors attacked the area, killing, looting and burning the homes of Kikuyus and Luhyas. The Kalenjin community in the area justified the attack by stating that Kikuyus had been pressuring them to join the political opposition.[49] In retaliation, Kikuyu youth began to stone passing cars on the road. By the time the fighting subsided twenty-four hours later, the fire had spread over an area of approximately twenty by thirty kilometers. A week before the fighting, the Uasin Gishu district commissioner had reportedly said at a public meeting that "in Kenyatta's days, if a Luhya had said something against the Kikuyu he would be killed, so now why should Kikuyus say things against the Kalenjin."[50] Throughout the month of December, the fighting raged in Uasin Gishu.

By the time the election was held on December 29, 1992, thousands of Kenyans were unable to cast their ballot as a result of the displacement and destruction caused by the ethnic clashes. Many eligible voters had lost property titles or identification that would have enabled them to register to vote. Others were unable to return to their home areas to vote. The Commonwealth election observer team cited the ethnic violence as a major impediment to a free and fair election stating their

> strong concern about the reports of numerous cases of violence and land clashes which marred the period immediately preceding polling day and which

---

[48] Interview with Kalenjin (Kipsigis) woman, Olenguruone, Nakuru District, June 25, 1993.

[49] Interview with Kalenjin (Nandi) clash victim, Kondoo Farm, Burnt Forest, Uasin Gishu District, June 29, 1993.

[50] Interview with Fr. Peter Elungata, Burnt Forest Catholic church, Eldoret, Uasin Gishu District, June 29, 1993.

exacerbated the distrust which prevailed among tribal groups, other communities and the political parties. Members of our Group were made very much aware of the pervasive effects of the violence, particularly in the Rift Valley, and were able to gain a ready appreciation of the volatility of the areas where violence had occurred.[51]

GOVERNMENT RESPONSE TO THE PRE-ELECTION VIOLENCE

From the outset, the government's response to the violence was grossly inadequate. The government and local administration authorities attempted to play down the conflict by blaming the opposition and the press for blowing the issue out of proportion. Later, they blamed the opposition for organizing the violence. In March 1992, an unsigned, undated statement was released by the government claiming that the political opposition was responsible for instigating the clashes through the recruitment of a Libyan-trained terrorist squad. The government accused the opposition of planning to sabotage vital installations and impersonate the regular police force. The government also accused the opposition of infiltrating the press, which "continues to constantly and selectively highlight these atrocities and deliberately attribute them to the government."[52] During the same month, President Moi banned all political rallies, citing the ethnic clashes as the reason. He also blamed the press for "spreading lies" and threatened to enact banning orders against such newspapers.[53] Periodically, the government put out statements calling for the violence to end. However, little was done to deploy adequate security or to provide assistance or relief to the victims of the violence.

---

[51] Commonwealth Secretariat, *The Presidential, Parliamentary and Civic Elections in Kenya*, The Report of the Commonwealth Observer Group, December 29, 1992, p. 23.

[52] "New Spate of Violence," *Weekly Review*, March 13, 1992, p. 19.

[53] "Getting to Grips with Tragedy," *Weekly Review*, March 27, 1992, p. 11.

Often, Kalenjin attackers who were arrested were reported to have been released the following day without charge.[54] In March 1992, the Office of the President released a statement revealing that 700 people had been arrested for the violence.[55] Weeks later, the police said that, in fact, half that number had been arrested. They gave no explanation for the discrepancy in the figures.[56] No further mention was ever made of the opposition's supposed Libyan-trained recruits.

GOVERNMENT INVOLVEMENT IN THE CLASHES

As the death toll continued to rise, most Kenyans agreed that the outbreak of the violence was linked to the transition to a multi-party system. However, speculation continued as to whether the violence was a spontaneous response to the political upheaval or instigated by the government to prove its prediction that ethnic violence would be the result of a change to multi-partyism.

Increasingly, allegations of direct government involvement in the clashes began to surface. In April 1992, a report entitled *The Cursed Arrow* was released by the National Council of Churches of Kenya (NCCK) that linked the violence to high-ranking government officials.[57] The report cited the license numbers of two Isuzu trucks, registered in the name of a Member of Parliament, that were seen transporting armed warriors. The NCCK report concluded,

> These clashes were and are politically motivated . . . to achieve through violence what was not achieved in the political platform, i.e., forcing *majimboism* on the Kenyan people. Here the strategy being to create a situation on the ground for a possible political bargain in the debate about the system of government in future Kenya.

---

[54] "A Story of Indelible Damage," *Weekly Review*, March 20, 1992, p. 12.

[55] "Ethnic Strife," *Weekly Review*, March 20, 1992, p. 7.

[56] "The Slaughter of Two Schoolgirls," *Weekly Review*, March 27, 1992, p. 13.

[57] NCCK, *The Cursed Arrow: Organized Violence Against Democracy in Kenya*, April 1992.

Obviously, one of the consequences of the clashes is slowing down of the current democratization process. With the clashes, energies and focus have been redirected and ethnicity has become an important factor in the political debate.[58]

The same month, a report was released by a task force formed of representatives from the NCCK, the political opposition parties, the International Commission of Jurists (ICJ-Kenya), the Law Society of Kenya (LSK), the University of Nairobi, and the Women's Lobby Group. The task force had been set up following an inter-party symposium in May 1992. The purpose of the report was to investigate the causes of the violence and to make recommendations for helping the victims. The report stated that the attacks were organized under a central command, often in the presence of local administration and security officers and that warriors who were arrested were often released unconditionally. The task force report mentioned that high-ranking government officials, including MP Nicholas Biwott, had paid warriors in return for the destruction they caused. The report concluded that the violence had resulted in the displacement of 50,000.[59]

The most damning indictment of direct government involvement in the clashes came from the report of an official Parliamentary Select Committee, set up in May 1992 as a way of diverting the growing public outrage over the issue. Then-speaker of the National Assembly Jonathan Ng'eno had blocked discussion of the clashes in Parliament four times and finally agreed to the formation of a Select Committee after several MPs threatened a mass walk-out.[60] The thirteen-member Parliamentary Committee, chaired by MP for Changamwe, Kennedy Kiliku, travelled around the country conducting extensive interviews.[61] Since Kenya was

---

[58] NCCK, *The Cursed Arrow*, p. 1.

[59] Inter-Parties *Symposium I Task Force Report*, June 11, 1992.

[60] "The Clashes Report," *Weekly Review*, September 25, 1992, p. 3.

[61] The Committee consisted of J. Kennedy Kiliku, Bahati M. Semo, P.P.L. Angelei, Mwacharo Kubo, J. Muruthi Mureithi, F.T. Lagat, Agnes M. Ndetei, Bob F. Jalang'o, G.K. Parsaoti, J.J. Falana, Zedekiah M. Magara, Wasike Ndombi, and

still under one-party rule at the time, all the Parliamentary Select
Committee members were KANU MPs.

In September 1992, the Committee released a 238-page report,
which verified that the attacks, far from being spontaneous, were
politically motivated and had been orchestrated by Kalenjin and Maasai
individuals close to the President, including Vice-President George Saitoti
and MPs Ezekiel Barngetuny and Nicholas Biwott. The Kiliku Report,
as it came to be known, supported the widely held public view that
government administrators abetted the violence. The Kiliku Report
concluded that the violence had been instigated "in the misconception that
some ethnic communities could chase away other ethnic communities in
order to acquire their land." The Committee found that numerous
Kalenjin government officials and security officers had contributed to the
violence. Many of the names cited in the report as being behind the
organization and funding of the "warriors" had been involved in the
majimbo rallies. The report noted that

> Evidence received by the Committee . . . indicates that
> the fighters were on hire and were paid sums ranging
> from Kshs. 500 [US $6.50] for safe return from the clash
> front, Kshs. 1,000 to 2,000 [US $12.50 to $25] for killing
> one person or burning a grass-thatched house and Kshs.
> 10,000 [US $125] per permanent house burnt. Several
> witnesses also alleged that some of the persons funding
> the wages of the "warriors" were the Hon. K.N.K. Biwott,
> EGH, MP; the Hon. Rueben K. Chesire, MP; the Hon.
> Ezekiel K. Barngetuny, MP; the proprietor of Guest
> House at Kedowa market, Kipkelion division; and the
> Hon. Wilson Leitich, MP.[62]

The report also noted that many of the warriors were actually
transported by vehicles, including government cars, to and from the clash
areas, citing the vehicles involved, their registration numbers and their

Mohamed Sheikh Aden. Republic of Kenya, *Report of the Parliamentary Select
Committee to investigate Ethnic Clashes in Western and Other Parts of Kenya*, p. (v).

[62] Republic of Kenya, *Report of the Parliamentary Select Committee to investigate
Ethnic Clashes in Western and Other Parts of Kenya*, p. 75.

owners. In some cases, government helicopters had transported the warriors. The Committee unanimously agreed that the provincial administration and security forces, by often refusing to assist clash victims and releasing attackers who had been arrested, did not react to the situation with the required urgency.

The report estimated that by September 1992, the violence had caused the deaths of 779 people, injured 600 people, rendered as many as 56,000 families homeless and resulted in property damage of over Kshs. 210 million [US $2,625,000]. The report recommended that "appropriate action be taken against those administration officials who directly or indirectly participated or encouraged the clashes," naming Nicholas Biwott and Ezekiel Barngetuny in particular. The report also recommended an ethnic balance in the appointment of administrative and security personnel and the creation of a Special Trust Fund to assist victims. On October 14, 1992, the Kiliku Report was rejected by Parliament. Three members of the Select Parliamentary Committee, who had signed and endorsed the report, voted against it.[63]

At the same time, *Finance* magazine ran a cover story on "Biwott's Private Army," which was promptly impounded by the police.[64] The issue contained a copy of a sworn affidavit by a Kalenjin man by the name of Valentinus Uhuru Kodipo (alias Abdul Kadir arap Kigen) who had given information to the Kiliku Committee during the course of their investigation. Mr. Kodipo claimed to have been recruited into a private army formed by Nicholas Biwott. In the affidavit, Mr. Kodipo swore that

> in October 1991 we were given thorough rough briefings to the effect that the Rift Valley Province must be cleared and people from other provinces in Kenya removed and that the multi-party system must not be allowed to succeed . . . that private army in these camps, we were told, would be called the Kalenjin warriors, and if Moi was defeated in the election, the army could be called the Kalenjin Liberation Front Army . . . that at the camps we were trained by the GSU and anti-stock theft unit personnel and there were regular visits by people like

---

[63] NEMU, *Courting Disaster*, April 29, 1993, p. 8.

[64] "Kalenjin Liberation Army," *Finance*, September 15, 1992, p. 20-26.

Captain Belsoi, Nicholas Biwott, George Saitoti, [William] ole Ntimama, [Kipkalia] Kones, [Ezekiel] Barngetuny and others . . . On January 6, 1992, we were mobilized for the Sondu operation consisting of sixteen gunmen and ninety personnel armed with fire and poisoned arrows . . . the personnel armed with arrows set fire on huts and houses in Nyakach and shot and killed people as they came out of their houses and huts . . . that after the Sondu operation we were told other major operations would follow in Molo and other places and I participated in similar operations in the areas around Songhor, Chemili and Muhoroni . . . that sometime in March 1992 I decided to escape from the camp in the Maasai Mara because I could not be party any longer to these massacres and destruction.[65]

---

[65] "Affidavit of Valentinus Uhuru Kodipo of Kadere, Nyanza Province sworn August 13, 1992," as reported in *Finance*, September 15, 1992, p. 22.

4. THE VIOLENCE CONTINUES
AFTER THE ELECTION

Since the election in December 1992, the ethnic violence has shown no sign of ending. Large organized attacks by Kalenjin warriors continue in some areas. In other areas, acts of intimidation and violence are targeted at individuals who attempt to return to their land. Increasingly, the large-scale attacks appear to be affecting Kikuyus rather than other ethnic groups. In April 1993, the National Election Monitoring Unit (NEMU), a local organization set up initially to monitor the election, published a report entitled *Courting Disaster* on the continuing violence following the election. The report noted "the successful use of [traditional] warriors in this violence is now becoming a strategy to counter anti-government sentiments"[66] and that the Districts worst affected included Uasin Gishu, Trans Nzoia, Bungoma, and Nakuru.

UASIN GISHU DISTRICT

According to NCCK relief officials, Uasin Gishu District (the home area of Nicholas Biwott) currently has the largest number of displaced people, predominantly Kikuyus, who have not been able to return to their land.[67] Most of them are scattered, living off the goodwill of neighbors and friends. A news report on the violence in Uasin Gishu read:

> Of all the violence that has been perpetrated in the Rift in recent times, that of Burnt Forest near Eldoret has had the most profound effect on the people. That is because the clashes have been on and off. After the warriors leave, the people discuss the issue and think the matter is over, but the warriors return soon and the

---

[66] NEMU, *Courting Disaster*, April 29, 1993, p. 21.

[67] Interview with Ephraim Kiragu, NCCK outreach director, Nairobi, June 18, 1993.

whole vicious cycle starts all over again. The people are
so scared even to trust their neighbors.[68]

The Burnt Forest area in Uasin Gishu has been hit particularly
hard. The area was attacked in December 1992 and again in January
1993. Four people were killed after approximately 300 warriors armed
with bows and arrows attacked Rukini and Kondoo farms. A few days
later, ten houses were set ablaze in Lorian trading center, where refugees
from Lorian farm had sought refuge following violence in December
1992. On February 4, 1993, 200 warriors armed with bows and arrows
attacked Ya Mumbi trading center near Burnt Forest. The police arrived
at the scene seven hours after the attack began, despite the fact that they
were stationed only six kilometers away. In April 1993, there was a
second attack on another settlement farm, Lokwania farm, by Kalenjins.
       Few victims in Uasin Gishu have been able to return to their
farms. Rironi Farm, one of the settlement farms attacked in December
1992, has been occupied illegally by Kalenjin farmers who have renamed
it Kaplelach.[69] At Kondoo farm, a Kalenjin man told Africa Watch that
before the violence, the number of Kikuyus was much higher than that
of the Kalenjins, but that since the violence, the number has been about
equal.[70] Africa Watch visited Liangushe camp, a market center where
approximately 300 Kikuyu clash victims driven off Kondoo farm were
seeking refuge in approximately eight small buildings. They had been
unable to return to their land. The NCCK knows of only three farms
where people have successfully resettled in Uasin Gishu--all three cases
were of Kalenjins who had been driven off their land in retaliatory
attacks by Kikuyus in the area.[71]

---

[68] "Neighbour Turns on Neigbour," *Daily Nation*, May 10, 1993, Part V - Life
in the Clash Areas series.

[69] NEMU, *Courting Disaster*, April 29, 1993, p. 14.

[70] Interview with Kalenjin farmer, Kondoo farm III, Burnt Forest, Uasin
Gishu District, June 29, 1993.

[71] Interview with Pastor Samson Khalwale, NCCK District Office, Eldoret,
Uasin Gishu District, June 29, 1993.

In August 1993, Kalenjins attacked the Burnt Forest area again. One attack resulted in the deaths of five Kikuyus. Residents of Kamuyu farm in Burnt Forest complained that the Chief of Laingushe location was aware of the names of the attackers but that nothing had been done.[72]

TRANS NZOIA AND BUNGOMA DISTRICTS

The violence in the Trans Nzoia and Bungoma Districts has predominantly affected the Luhya community. The Kalenjin warriors who launched attacks in these districts have used guns in addition to bows and arrows. There is strong Kalenjin (Sabaot) nationalist sentiment in this area and the Sabaot community in the Mt. Elgon sub-district area has been calling for the government to redraw district boundary lines to give Sabaots their own district. Accordingly, they have been intimidating and pressuring non-Kalenjins to leave the area, from Chwele (Bungoma District) to Saboti (Trans Nzoia District).[73] In January and February 1993, there were a number of attacks which left over fourteen Luhyas dead.

Most clash victims in these two districts are living in dismal conditions in camps or market centers. In Trans Nzoia District, victims in the largest refugee camp at Endebess were dispersed forcibly by local government authorities. At Kolongolo, Trans Nzoia, Africa Watch interviewed Luhya victims at the market center where they have been since their homes were attacked by Kalenjins (Pokots) in March and December 1992. One Luhya victim told Africa Watch,

> People have not gone back because they are afraid and
> their homes are destroyed. They do not have any money
> to build new homes. They go back to cultivate during
> the day, but the Kalenjins graze their cattle on our land

---

[72] "Armed Raiders Kill Two," *Daily Nation*, August 26, 1993.

[73] "The Fuse Burns Low in Bungoma and Trans Nzoia Districts," *Daily Nation*, May 8, 1993, Part IV - Life in the Clash Areas series.

and steal things, and if we tell them to move, they threaten to attack us.[74]

In Bungoma District, there are large numbers of displaced persons in camps. Africa Watch visited Kapkateny camp, where approximately 2,000 Luhyas had fled when they were attacked in April 1992. The attack left over ten people dead, seven injured and over 2,000 houses burned. Over time, the number of people living at Kapkateny has decreased to one hundred as people have sought shelter elsewhere. In a one-room shed of approximately twenty by sixty feet, the displaced population lives in cramped, unhygienic conditions. People have been eating nothing but potatoes and maize meal given by the churches. Kalenjins (Sabaots) are now occupying the land which they used to farm on.[75] Africa Watch also visited a camp at Namwela where approximately 140 victims have lived since Kalenjins attacked them in April 1992. One Luhya man told Africa Watch that he has been harassed by Kalenjins when he has tried to return to his land.

NAKURU DISTRICT

Nakuru District, site of the provincial capital, Nakuru, has remained volatile since the violence began in February 1992. Throughout 1993, the violence has continued unabated. Travelling through the Olenguruone area of Nakuru District, Africa Watch saw large tracts of deserted and abandoned farmland. Most of the Kikuyu residents who used to live on those farms have sought refuge in Elburgon or Kamwaura camps. On May 26, 1993, the Kisii community remaining in Olenguruone were threatened through anonymous leaflets stating that if they did not move from Olenguruone they would have "their heads chopped off" within a week's time.[76]

---

[74] Interview with Luhya clash victim, Kolongolo, Trans Nzoia District, June 30, 1993.

[75] Interview with Luhya clash victim, Kapkateny, Bungoma District, July 1, 1993.

[76] "Leaflets Back," *Daily Nation*, May 28, 1993.

Ernest Murimi of the Catholic Justice and Peace Commission estimated to Africa Watch in June 1993 that over 40,000 people had been displaced in the Nakuru area, most of whom are Kikuyu. He noted that the attackers had become so brazen that they had begun to attack in broad daylight, without any fear of being arrested.[77]

Africa Watch visited the camps at Elburgon and Kamwaura where the living conditions of the displaced population are appalling. Shelter and food at both camps are being provided by the Catholic church. At Kamwaura camp, over 500 displaced people are living, sleeping, and cooking in a one-room church hall. There are six pit latrines and one tap, which the church has installed outside. The government has not given any assistance.

In May 1993, Nakuru town, the Provincial capital of Rift Valley Province was hit by four days of rioting after police demolished without notice 600 kiosks that housed predominantly Kikuyu local street hawkers.[78] The demolition was seen by many Kenyans as an extension of the ethnic clashes and another way for the government to intimidate and disempower the Kikuyu population in Rift Valley Province.

In August 1993, approximately 300 Kalenjin warriors armed with bows and arrows attacked Molo, sparking off another month of violence in the area.[79] Hundreds of Kikuyus fled to Kenjoketty, about twenty kilometers away. Victims at Kenjoketty claimed that Kalenjins had attacked and selectively torched over 200 houses belonging to Kikuyus for four consecutive days. The police in the area took no action.[80]

---

[77] Interview with Ernest Murimi, Executive Secretary, Justice and Peace Commission, Catholic Diocese of Nakuru, Nakuru District, June 24, 1993.

[78] "Who Should Know if Not the PC?" *Daily Nation*, May 11, 1993.

[79] "3 More Killed in Rising Violence," *Daily Nation*, August 26, 1993.

[80] "Fifteen Killed in New Clashes Says Mungai," *Daily Nation*, August 22, 1993.

SECURITY OPERATION ZONES

On September 2, 1993, President Moi declared "security operation zones" in Molo (Nakuru District), Burnt Forest (Uasin Gishu District) and Londiani (Kericho District). Under the Constitution, the President has powers to seal off any part of the country when public order is threatened. Section 85 of the Constitution gives the President powers to invoke Part III of the Preservation of Public Security Act by an order published in the Kenya Gazette. Part III of the Preservation of Public Security Act allows the President, among other things, to regulate and restrict the movement of persons, censor the press and prohibit any meetings or processions, in any part of Kenya. The Constitution further states that

> such order under this section shall cease to have effect on the expiration of a period of 28 days commencing with the day on which the order is made where before the expiration of that period it has been approved by a resolution of the National Assembly.[81]

To date, the presidential order declaring the security operation zones has not been approved by Parliament. Accordingly, Kenyan lawyers argue that these security operation zones have been unconstitutional since October 1, 1993.

The areas designated security operation zones were immediately sealed off by paramilitary troops from the General Service Unit (GSU) who barred entry to all outsiders. Shortly afterwards, Minister for Information and Broadcasting Johnstone Makau warned that the government would discipline any media person who "misreported sensitive issues" in the clash areas.[82]

The legality of the government's actions and its motive were immediately challenged by concerned Kenyans who were worried that the government might misuse the restrictions on movement to commit atrocities against non-Kalenjins inside the zones. Opposition politicians

---

[81] Constitution of Kenya.

[82] "Press Faces Curbs on Clash Issues," *Standard*, September 6, 1993.

also objected to the restrictions on press in the area, stating that the "sealing-off of the areas is meant as an information black-out."[83]

The announcement came shortly after two visits by representatives of Western organizations to the Molo region, one by Lord David Ennals of the British Refugee Council and the other by Kerry Kennedy-Cuomo, executive director of the Robert F. Kennedy Memorial Center for Human Rights. Both had criticized the government's role in the violence. Lord Ennals had denounced the violence, stating that "the government and law and order agencies have done nothing to stop this policy which resembles ethnic cleansing in Bosnia." He also commented that it was "a terrible indictment of Kenyan leaders that they are ready to instigate violence and death to prove that democracy does not work." Ms. Kennedy-Cuomo concluded that the Kenyan government had "failed to guarantee protection to its citizens regardless of their political convictions or affiliation."[84]

Since designation of the security operation zones, a number of people have been arrested. However, many of them have not been Kalenjin warriors. Thirteen opposition MPs were arrested and charged with breaching the peace when they attempted to enter the area on a fact-finding mission.[85] Days later, Bedan Mbugua, editor of *The People*, and Rev. Timothy Njoya were arrested when they attempted to visit Molo and were held in police custody for three days. Nakuru Senior Principal Magistrate William Tuiyot said that he was too tired to hear listen to the bail application when they were brought into court on September 10, 1993, and charged with obstructing the police and organizing an illegal procession. PCEA Rev. Johnson Muhia Nyutu was also arrested after he went to retrieve Rev. Njoya's car at the police roadblock.[86] A group of musicians that made a recording of songs about the violence were

---

[83] "FORD-K Officials Want Press Allowed into Molo," *Daily Nation*, September 6, 1993.

[84] "Kenyan Government Seals off Tribal Battle Grounds," *Agence France Presse*, September 22, 1993 available in LEXIS, Nexis library.

[85] "Clashes: 13 MPs on Demo Charge" and "13 Opposition MPs in Court," *Daily Nation*, September 4, 1993.

[86] "Njoya Arrested at Elburgon," *Daily Nation*, September 11, 1993.

declared wanted for arrest by the police. The songs had been written to raise money for the victims of the violence. Vendors who have attempted to sell the cassette tape have been harassed by the police.[87] In Burnt Forest, Uasin Gishu District, a Kikuyu farmer, Nelson Wambugu Kinga, was charged with being in possession of a seditious publication--five photographs of clash victims.[88]

On September 18, 1993, five people were arrested in the Burnt Forest security operation zone, for being in possession of seditious literature and illegal weapons. Among those arrested were a prominent government critic Koigi wa Wamwere and lawyer Mirugi Kariuki. Both Mr. Wamwere and Mr. Kariuki had been arrested and held on treason charges from September 1990 to January 1993 during which time they were ill-treated. The allegedly seditious publications in their possession included leaflets published by the National Democratic and Human Rights Organization (NDEHURIO) founded recently by Mr. Wamwere. NDEHURIO had taken up the issue of the ethnic clashes. The illegal weapons allegedly in their possession included a rifle, a grenade and fifteen rounds of ammunition. They were also accused of entering the restricted security zone in Burnt Forest. Three others were arrested later that day at the homes of Mssrs. Wamwere and Kariuki in Nakuru. All eight prisoners were held incommunicado by the police in Nakuru and denied access to a lawyer for four days.[89] On September 22, 1993, seven of the eight were brought into court in Nakuru where they refused to plead to the charges, complained of being beaten by the police, and denied being in possession of weapons. The eighth prisoner, John Kinyanjui, was released unconditionally. By October 11, 1993, all eight had been released on bail. Additional charges of "administering an

---

[87] *See* Article 19, *Kenya: Shooting the Messenger*, October 29, 1993.

[88] "Njoya Arrested at Elburgon," *Daily Nation*, September 11, 1993.

[89] Amnesty International, *Urgent Action*, AFR 32/12/93, September 21, 1993. The others arrested included Susan Wangui (Mr. Kariuki's wife); Francis Mureithi Kanothe (a farmer); Joseph Thiga Kariuki (Mr. Kariuki's brother); Geoffrey Kuria Kariuki (Mr. Wamwere's cousin and former treason trialist); John Njoroge (Mr. Wamwere's brother); and John Kinyanjui (member of Release Political Prisoners campaign).

unlawful oath" were brought against Mssrs. Wamwere and Kariuki.[90] Another sixty Kikuyus have also been arrested for reportedly taking part in an illegal oathing ceremony.[91]

Other observers who have attempted to provide relief or monitor events in the security operation zones have been stopped by the government. On September 3, 1993, a Red Cross food convoy containing seven tons of grain intended for clash victims was barred entry into Molo by security forces. A group of Dutch Parliamentarians visiting Kenya were also prohibited access to the Molo area on September 6, 1993. The Parliamentarians were there to gather information on which to base future relations with the Kenya. A journalist from the *Daily Nation* was evicted from the Molo area for trying to report on relief activities. On September 5, 1993, at Molo Hospital, police confiscated cameras from two journalists, Raphael Munge, a *Standard* photographer, and Joseph Ngugi, a *Daily Nation* reporter, after they took pictures of hospitalized clash victims.[92]

The government was quick to claim that it had ended the ethnic violence with its creation of the three security operation zones. However, on October 12, 1993, clashes broke out south of the security operation zones in Enosupukia, Narok District. Houses of Kikuyus at Gatima farm were torched by Maasais in the early morning, leaving four dead. Police reinforcements were deployed in the area; however, the violence has continued.[93] On October 15, 1993, approximately 500 armed men wearing traditional Maasai dress (*shukas*) carrying knives and sharpened sticks attacked Enosupukia. Kikuyus who sought refuge from the attackers in the near by Mission Church were also attacked by the Maasais. The district officer ordered the police reinforcements that had been sent to Enosupukia to return to Nakuru District on the grounds that

---

[90] Amnesty International, *Urgent Action*, AFR 32/14/93, October 11, 1993.

[91] "Police Detain 61 for Ethnic Violence in Rift Valley," BBC World Service, September 26, 1993 as reported in Foreign Broadcast Information Service *Daily Report* (FBIS) Afr/93/186, September 28, 1993, p. 5.

[92] "Mukaru is Arrested in Molo," *Standard*, September 5, 1993.

[93] "Police Reinforcements Dispatched Following Reported Killings and Theft," KBC Radio, October 25, 1993 as reported in SWB AL/1830 A/6, October 27, 1993.

Narok District was not their area of jurisdiction. After the police left, there was a second attack which left seventeen Kikuyus dead. The Catholic church estimated that the clashes had left 30,000 people displaced. The government has not provided any food relief for the displaced. As of October 26, 1993, attacks were still continuing in Narok District and large areas of land remained deserted by the thousands of Kikuyus who have fled in fear for their lives.[94]

Outraged opposition politicians immediately brought the issue of the renewed violence into Parliament as an issue of urgent national importance, and named Narok MP William ole Ntimama as the instigator of the Enosupukia violence. Mr. Ntimama responded to the charges in Parliament by saying that he had "no regrets about the events in Enosupukia because the Maasai were fighting for their rights." He also said in Parliament that the Kikuyu "had suppressed the Maasai, taken their land and degraded their environment . . . . We had to say enough is enough. I had to lead the Maasai in protecting our rights."[95] Attempts by forty-one members of the opposition to demand the dismissal of ole Ntimama by President Moi was voted down by fifty-eight KANU MPs on October 22, 1993.[96]

The flare-up of violence in Narok District, which has left over twenty Kikuyus dead, indicates that Kenyans have not seen the end of the clashes yet.

---

[94] Catholic Diocese of Ngong, *Press Release* by Fr. Dominic Waweru, Chair, Justice and Peace Commission, October 26, 1993.

[95] "Minister: 'No Regrets' Over Events," *Daily Nation*, October 20, 1993, as reported in FBIS Afr/93/202, October 21, 1993, p. 8.

[96] "Opposition Ultimatum for Dismissal of Local Government Minister Rejected," KBC Radio, October 22, 1991, as reported in SWB AL/1830/ A/6, October 27, 1993.

THE GOVERNMENT'S RESPONSE

5. GOVERNMENT INACTION

All governments have a universally recognized obligation to ensure that their citizens are free from extra-legal or arbitrary killings. Article 6 of the International Covenant on Civil and Political Rights (the International Covenant), guarantees every human being the inherent right to life and states that "[t]his right shall be protected by law. No one shall be arbitrarily deprived of his life." Kenya has ratified the International Covenant and has a legal obligation to guarantee this rights.

Governments also have a duty to prosecute serious violations of physical integrity under international law. Article 26 of the International Covenant guarantees:

> All persons are equal before the law and are entitled without any discrimination to the equal protection of the law. In this respect, the law shall prohibit any discrimination and guarantee to all persons equal and effective protection against discrimination on any ground such as race, colour, sex, language, religion, political or other opinion, national or social origin, property, birth or other status.

The UN Human Rights Committee, which monitors the compliance of all state parties with the International Covenant, has further held that the state not only has a duty to protect its citizens from such violations, but also to investigate violations when they occur and to bring the perpetrators to justice.[97] To ensure effective implementation, the UN Economic and Social Council in 1989 adopted the Basic Principles on the Effective Prevention and Investigation of Extra-Legal, Arbitrary and Summary Executions. Principle 9 states:

---

[97] *See* Report of the Human Rights Committee, 37 UN GAOR Supp. (No. 40) Annex V, general comment 7(16), para 1 (1982) UN Doc. A/37/40(1982).

[There] shall be a thorough, prompt and impartial investigation of all suspected cases of extra-legal, arbitrary and summary executions, including cases where complaints by relatives and other reliable reports suggest unnatural deaths. Governments shall maintain investigative offices and procedures to undertake such inquiries. The purpose of the investigation shall be to determine the cause, manner and time of death, the person responsible and any pattern or practice which may have brought about that death.[98]

NO SECURITY OR POLICE PROTECTION

The Kenyan police and security forces have done little to protect the victims of the violence. Victims have consistently complained of the partiality of law enforcement officers sent to stop the clashes. Noting the government's inaction, the NCCK pointed out in April 1992, that:

While it took the law enforcement forces only a few days to crush peaceful demonstrators in Nairobi who were only urging the government to release political prisoners, nothing has so far been done to quell the clashes which have now entered their sixth month.[99]

In many cases, victims have complained that police officers stood by and watched while Kalenjin warriors attacked. In other cases, the police have refused to accept statements from witnesses trying to report an incident. In March 1992, two journalists in the Londiani area came across dead

---

[98] Principles on the Effective Prevention and Investigation of Extra-Legal, Arbitrary and Summary Executions, adopted by the Economic and Social Council, May 24, 1989, *reprinted in* "Report by the Special Rapporteur Mr. S. Amos Wako, pursuant to the Economic and Social Council resolution 1988/38," Commission on Human Rights, Economic and Social Council, E/CN.4/1990/22, January 23, 1990.

[99] NCCK, *The Cursed Arrow*, p. 4.

bodies and burned houses. When they tried to report the situation to the police, the police denied that it had occurred.[100]

The police have also refused to investigate continuing acts of intimidation against non-Kalenjin individuals who attempt to return to their land. In Olenguruone, Nakuru District, a Kikuyu man who had been displaced from his land in April 1992 by Kalenjin attackers, tried to return to his farm a year later to plant. "As I began to hoe," he told Africa Watch,

> I looked up and saw four men coming towards me. They wore shorts and tee-shirts and their faces were covered. They were all armed with pangas. As they approached, I dropped my tools and ran. They took all my tools and went back into the forest area. I reported the incident to the police and gave a statement, but nothing was done. I have not gone back to my land since.[101]

Another Kikuyu woman from the same area, who has been living in an unused shed with approximately 500 other displaced victims at the Catholic Church compound at Kamwaura, Nakuru District, told Africa Watch that she had been chased away from her plot of land at Burone farm twice in June 1993. On both occasions, as soon as she began to plant, a man appeared from the nearby brush and ran towards her. Both times she fled, fearing for her life. That her fears were not unfounded is shown by the cases of two women who attempted to return to farm and were gang-raped in January and on May 28, 1993 respectively. Both cases were reported to the police, but no action was taken.[102] In Trans Nzoia District, Luhya clash victims told Africa Watch of similar instances of intimidation by Kalenjins when they tried to return to their land. A Luhya man who tried to return to his land to plant at Kalaha

---

[100] Interviews with Ngumo wa Kuria, Nakuru Bureau Chief, *Standard*, and Michael Njuguna, Nakuru reporter, *Nation*, Nakuru, June 24, 1993.

[101] Interview with Kikuyu clash victim, Kamwaura, Nakuru District, June 25, 1993.

[102] Interview with group of Kikuyu women clash victims, Kamwaura camp, Nakuru District, June 25, 1993.

farm in June 1992 was accosted by eight Sabaot Kalenjins who threatened to shoot him with arrows if he continued. Another Teso man from the same farm tried to return to rebuild his house in January 1993. When he returned the following day, he found it burned down. The police have not taken any action against the perpetrators of these crimes.[103]

There have been allegations, supported by statements of some junior policemen, that police officers are acting under orders not to shoot at Kalenjin attackers. The police have also complained that they are never deployed in sufficient numbers to stop fighting in the clash areas and, as a result, that they are at risk. They also point out that if they shoot at a Kalenjin warrior, they might just wound him and he will survive, but if they are hit by a poisoned arrow, they will immediately die. A respected Kenyan told Africa Watch confidentially that he had personally spoken to the Police Commissioner who had confirmed that he was receiving orders from "high up" and that "his hands are tied." When asked how high up, the Police Commissioner apparently said "from the highest place."[104] Ernest Murimi, Executive Secretary of the Catholic Justice and Peace Commission, said to Africa Watch that because of the impunity that the attackers enjoy, they were now attacking in broad daylight even in the presence of the security forces and openly threatened to return in the future. He also reiterated his suspicion that the police had been given orders not to shoot, pointing out that in some cases the police had pleaded with the attackers not to burn and loot, but had not stopped the warriors.

On June 24, 1993, Africa Watch visited Londiani, Kericho District, two days after approximately 400 Kalenjin warriors launched an attack on the area. The after-effects of the violence were evident. The areas immediately affected were deserted except for a few of the victims who were milling about the charred remains of their houses. The burned buildings were still smoldering. The local school had been indefinitely closed, leaving approximately 500 children out of school. Other schools in the surrounding area were also closed. The attack had resulted in the death of at least one person, Michael Manguni, and another person had

---

[103] Interviews with Luhya and Teso clash victims, Mt. Elgon National Park camp, Trans Nzoia District, June 30, 1993.

[104] Interview (name withheld on request), Nairobi, July 13, 1993.

been injured. The lack of response by the police during this incident is similar to police behavior reported in hundreds of other attacks.

The men who raided the town in broad daylight were all dressed in shorts and *khangas*[105] and armed with bows and arrows. The area is inhabited by both Kikuyus and Kalenjins, but the warriors were careful only to burn down homes and buildings belonging to Kikuyus, leaving neighboring structures owned by Kalenjins intact. The home of the local Presbyterian priest, Rev. Solomon Kamau Macharia (a Kikuyu), had also been burned down. The Presbyterian Church of East Africa (PCEA) had been giving relief to victims from previous attacks in the area. The Maasai watchman guarding the PCEA property told Africa Watch

> The attackers spoke to each other in Kipsigis (one of the Kalenjin languages). When they saw me, they asked me in Kiswahili what tribe I was from and, when I said Maasai, they told me to get out. I am sure that if I had been Kikuyu they would have killed me. There were five armed police less than one hundred meters away standing at the fence of the compound watching the attackers loot and burn the building. I asked them for help, they didn't do anything except shoot a few times in the air. The attackers stayed for about one hour.[106]

A farmer who witnessed the attack also verified the police inaction as follows:

> I was working on my farm at around twelve noon when I heard children screaming from the nearby school. I came running from my *shaamba* [farm] and saw people running with bows and arrows. At first, I just saw two, and then some more came until there were about eight, and then another group of seven came from the other side. Eventually, there were about 400 men dressed in

---

[105] Local patterned cloth approximately three by five feet used for a variety of purposes from clothing to tablecloths.

[106] Interview with Maasai watchman at PCEA church house, Londiani, Kericho District, June 24, 1993.

shorts with no shirts and bows and arrows. They were splitting up into different groups on all sides and giving a battle cry. As people fled, the attackers shot some arrows. One barely missed me. There were five policemen at the site of the attack. They shot in the air but did not do anything else. In this compound, thirty people have been displaced--thirteen are children.[107]

People who had fled to the police station for shelter were chased away by the police.[108] When asked if anyone had reported the attack to the police, another victim of the attack, asked Africa Watch, "What for?"[109]

"The government's efforts to provide security have only been cosmetic," a diplomat told Africa Watch, "sometimes, for a short while there are extra policemen, but then they go." The lack of security has resulted in a complete lack of confidence in the government's ability to end the violence and has deterred victims from returning permanently to their land. "Even if it is relatively calm, people are afraid to go home and do not feel safe," the same diplomat continued,

Everything is quiet in the daytime, but attacks are at night. In the Mt. Elgon area, when people [mostly Luhya] have tried to return, they have been attacked-- and it only needs one attack for thousands of others to be deterred. Some people only dare to return to their areas in the daytime to work on their farms, and then leave at night.[110]

---

[107] Interview with Kikuyu clash victim, Londiani, Kericho District, June 24, 1993.

[108] Interview with Ivan Kariuki, journalist, Londiani, Kericho District, June 24, 1993.

[109] Interview with Kikuyu clash victim, Londiani, Kericho District, June 24, 1993.

[110] Interview with foreign diplomat (name withheld on request), Nairobi, June 18, 1993.

The government's recent decision to create "security operation zones" in Molo, Burnt Forest, and Londiani in September 1993 must be put into this context. The government has in the past deployed extra security forces for short periods of times to assert that it is taking action. However, never in the past two years has it undertaken a sustained program of action find a political solution to end the violence. These sporadic pockets of extra security will stop the violence in those areas only for as long as the extra security is deployed. In the meantime it will flare up elsewhere.

JUDICIAL APATHY

A disturbing aspect of the "ethnic" violence in Kenya has been the impunity enjoyed by Kalenjin attackers. The Kenyan judiciary appears unwilling or unable to punish speedily those responsible. This inaction on the part of the judiciary comes as no surprise. Human rights activists within Kenya and internationally have consistently identified the lack of an independent judiciary as a major obstacle to respect for human rights in Kenya.[111] The government has relied heavily on the judiciary to penalize its critics and, likewise, has allowed its supporters to evade legal sanctions.

The government claims that over 1,000 charges have been brought for crimes relating to the ethnic violence.[112] The Attorney-General told Africa Watch in July 1993 that the charges had led to 582

---

[111] *See* Robert F. Kennedy Memorial Center for Human Rights, *Justice Enjoined: The State of the Judiciary in Kenya* (1992).

[112] The official government figure for arrests between October 1991 and December 1992 is 1,422: 672 Kalenjins, 430 Kikuyus, 146 Luhyas, ninety-nine Luos, twenty-three Tesos, twenty-three Kambas, sixteen Kisiis, ten Turkanas and three Maasais. Of those, 1,324 people were charged with offenses including murder, arson, robbery, unlawful meetings, inciting violence, conveying stolen goods, possession of illegal weapons, and stock theft. Of those charged, the government claims that the largest number were Kalenjin at 625. Others charged included 430 Kikuyus, ninety-nine Luhyas, ninety-nine Luos, twenty-three Tesos, thirteen Kambas, twelve Kisiis, ten Turkanas and three Maasais. The government figures given distinguish between the number of Kalenjins and Sabaots arrested. Since the Sabaot are usually considered Kalenjin, Africa Watch has joined the two numbers. Interview with Amos Wako, Attorney-General, Nairobi, July 12, 1993.

convictions (fines or jail sentences of four to fifteen years), 196 acquittals, 532 still pending and eight under investigation.[113]   However, Africa Watch found that many of these cases had not been pursued forcefully, and that most of those charged even with violent offenses were out on bail.   Africa Watch found that, contrary to government claims, where there have been convictions for possession of illegal weapons, a disproportionate number have been non-Kalenjins.   When asked about this imbalance, Attorney-General Amos Wako told Africa Watch, "Anyone with a weapon is arrested.   It doesn't matter which group.   We must arrest anyone with a weapon."[114]   In practice, however, hundreds of armed Kalenjin warriors have wreaked havoc and destruction on other ethnic communities without being arrested or charged for their actions. Executive Secretary of the Catholic Justice and Peace Commission Ernest Murimi told Africa Watch that, in Londiani, he had personally ensured that fifty-six people responsible for attacks were arrested and brought into court.   They had all been released without being charged.[115]

Attorney-General Amos Wako complained to Africa Watch that the number of prosecutions that could be brought was limited by the fact that victims did not complain to the police.   However, victims who attempted to report incidents of violence to the police have reported that the police have refused to take statements, or told them to go back to the place of the violence to file a statement.   Police have also been known to chase away displaced victims who sought refuge at the police station. These tactics have greatly reduced the likelihood of victims being able even to place these violations on the public record, much less prosecute those responsible for the violence.[116]   Yet the Attorney-General's Office has not taken steps to address this situation or to bring those responsible for the violations to book.

---

[113] Interview with Amos Wako, Attorney-General, Nairobi, July 12, 1993.

[114] Ibid.

[115] Interview with Ernest Murimi, Executive Secretary, Justice and Peace Commission, Catholic Diocese of Nakuru, Nakuru, June 24, 1993.

[116] Lawyers Committee for Human Rights, *Human Rights in Kenya and Malawi*, Testimony of Binaifer Nowrojee before the Subcommittee on African Affairs, U.S. House of Representatives, June 23, 1992.

DISCRIMINATORY APPLICATION OF THE LAW

Although the government seemingly has had difficulties in arresting and prosecuting Kalenjin warriors, it has efficiently and quickly prosecuted non-Kalenjins who have acquired weapons to defend themselves after being attacked.   While the government has valid concerns regarding the proliferation of weapons in the affected areas, it has adopted a selective policy in bringing prosecutions against non-Kalenjins for the possession of illegal weapons.

In February 1993, press reports indicated that the government had begun to prosecute people in the clash areas for possession of homemade guns. All those arrested were non-Kalenjins. A seventy-eight year old Kikuyu farmer from Burnt Forest, Uasin Gishu District, was jailed for four years on February 25, 1993, after pleading guilty to a charge of being in illegal possession of 117 rounds of ammunition. The defendant, Zablon Njuguna Kamau, stated that the arms were to be used to defend his family against attacks by Kalenjins.   In March, eleven people from the same area were charged with the illegal possession of seven homemade guns and ammunition.   They complained of having been badly beaten in police custody. According to a Catholic priest from the area, the eleven had organized their community to defend themselves from Kalenjin attacks earlier in the year.[117]

Given this discriminatory application of the law, the order by then-Chief Justice Alan Hancox to all magistrates to inform him of all cases where the government prosecutor did not oppose a bail application on charges of illegal possession of firearms or ammunition was all the more disturbing. The Chief Justice's circular was seemingly intended to put pressure on magistrates to deny bail for all people charged with firearms offenses. Kenyan lawyers opposed the circular on the grounds that it fettered the magistrate's discretionary powers to grant bail and had the effect of introducing through the back door detention without trial. The circular was eventually withdrawn.[118]   The government has adopted a similar policy of discriminatory application of the law with regard to statements made by politicians. While the government has been quick to accuse opposition politicians of making inflammatory

---

[117] NEMU, *Courting Disaster*, April 29, 1993, p. 19.

[118] Ibid.

statements about the clashes, it has been notably reticent in censuring its own KANU officials.

In July 1993, when opposition MP for Molo South, Njenga Mungai, whose area has been particularly hard hit by the violence, stated that Kikuyus should defend themselves from attacks, he was immediately arrested and interrogated. By contrast, no action has been taken against numerous KANU officials who have, for example, called for Kalenjins and Maasais to take up arms. In February 1993, Assistant Minister Sharif Nassir remarked that the clashes would continue as long as the opposition did not respect President Moi. In June 1993, the Mt. Elgon Member of Parliament, Wilberforce Kisiero, stated in Parliament that the ethnic clashes had been caused by "black colonialists" (Kikuyus) who had taken over land from the "indigenous" owners (Kalenjins and other pastoral groups) at independence.[119]

Minister for Local Government William ole Ntimama is renowned for his inflammatory comments, all of which have gone uncensured by the government. Before the election, Mr. Ntimama told all "outsiders" to leave Narok and warned Kikuyus in his area to "lie low like envelopes." He has also asserted that "non Maasais should not be allowed to vote" in his area (Narok District). In April 1993, he reportedly said "we will protect President Moi--do or die." Addressing his comments to "the original Rift Valley people," he called on Kalenjins and Maasais to "be ready to defend yourselves." In March 1993, he said that his district, Narok, would put the interests of the local people (the Maasai) first and the local council would give priority for hawker licenses to Maasais.[120] "We are not taking Ntimama's words for granted," a Kikuyu resident of Enosamplai, Narok District, said, "when he says people will die, they end up dying and we just have to take his threats very seriously."[121]

---

[119] "Ethnic Clashes 'Caused by Black Colonialists'," *Daily Nation*, June 24, 1993.

[120] "Quotable Quotes from the Honorable Minister," *The People*, June 6, 1993.

[121] "Why Ntimama Wants Kikuyus Out," *The People*, date unknown.

INADEQUATE RELIEF ASSISTANCE

Since the violence broke out, the government has made little or no effort to house or assist victims who are unable to return to their land. In a statement to Parliament in March 1992, almost six months after the violence broke out, Vice-President George Saitoti announced in Parliament that the government would provide food and other relief supplies valued at Kshs. 10 million [US $125,000] to the displaced clash victims.[122]

Such an amount would have been inadequate to resettle and compensate the hundreds of thousands of victims who had been made homeless. Unfortunately, even this paltry sum was never distributed to the victims. In the course of its investigation, Africa Watch was able to trace the distribution of only a tenth of this sum. The overwhelming majority of victims interviewed by Africa Watch had not received any assistance from the government. Distribution of relief assistance seemed to depend heavily on the honesty and efficiency of the local government officials in each area. It is not known what has happened to the remaining nine million shillings.

The only relief assistance given by the government that Africa Watch was able to verify was distributed at the following places:

- At Owiro farm in Nandi District, the government distributed Kshs. 200,000 [US $2,500] among the farm's 250 Luo shareholders in June 1993. Each family received approximately Kshs. 600 [US $7.50] per family. They also gave each family a ten kilogram bag of bean seeds to plant, and ploughed an acre of land for each family. However, the residents had to return Kshs. 40,000 [US $500] to the local government officials who charged them for ploughing the land.[123] One church relief worker noted that this relief coincided with a dialogue between President

---

[122] "Ethnic Strife," *Weekly Review*, March 20, 1992, p. 5.

[123] Interview with Luo clash victim, Owiro farm, Nandi District, July 2, 1993.

Moi and opposition leader Oginga Odinga (FORD-K) who is Luo, and speculated that the donation was given for that reason.[124]

- In Bungoma District, District Commissioner Rintari Kibiti told church relief workers that he had received Kshs. 400,000 [US $5,000] from the government for relief purposes, but that he was embarrassed because the amount was too small to assist effectively the large numbers of refugees in his district.[125] Some of the relief assistance was distributed to Kalenjin clash victims in Namwela by the District Officer in the form of blankets, food and money, the exact value of which is unknown.[126] In Kabuchai, another small group of Kalenjins in a predominantly Luhya area reportedly received tin sheets for roofing and potatoes.[127] In Cheptais, a Luhya community which had been attacked by Kalenjins received fifty kilograms of building nails and forty kilograms of maize seeds from the government in March 1993.[128] A nearby Kalenjin community which had been equally affected after a retaliatory attack by Luhyas had not received anything.[129]

- In Cherengani, Trans Nzoia District, the government gave food and tin sheets for roofing, valued at Kshs. 150,000 [US $1,875].[130]

---

[124] Interview with Moses Ote, NCCK relief coordinator, Nairobi, June 21, 1993.

[125] Ibid.

[126] Interview with Mukhisa Kituyi, FORD-K MP, Nairobi, July 9, 1993.

[127] Interview with Luhya victims at Sirisia, Bungoma District, July 1, 1993.

[128] Interview with old Luhya man, Kimaswa, Bungoma District, July 3, 1993.

[129] Interview with two young Kalenjin (Sabaot) men, Chepkube, Bungoma District, July 3, 1993.

[130] Interview (name withheld on request), Nairobi, July 13, 1993.

- At Elburgon, Nakuru District, the government provided 160 bags of sorghum, each containing ninety kilograms and estimated to be valued at Kshs. 144,000 [US $1,800]. The local authorities gave the food to the local Catholic church to distribute to Kikuyu and Kalenjin victims.[131]

- In Eldoret, Uasin Gishu District, the government distributed five to seven bags of maize meal at St. Matthews Church in December 1992.[132]

Although there have been allegations that the government money was distributed only to Kalenjin victims, Africa Watch found that in fact the few victims who received relief from the government were both Kalenjin and non-Kalenjin.

Another problem with government distribution of relief is that non-Kalenjin victims of the violence have a deep-rooted distrust of the government. Many believe that the clashes have been instigated by the government. Others have been badly treated by local government authorities who have attempted to force them to return to their land despite continuing attacks. As a result, many victims are suspicious of any government assistance and often will not accept it. In the Burnt Forest area, clash victims refused food that the government was distributing on December 14, 1992, on the grounds that it was poisoned.[133] "This distribution process requires a human face," a church relief worker told Africa Watch, "The situation is so polarized that people will only accept food from those that they trust."[134]

Most victims, Kalenjin and non-Kalenjin, currently receive food and other relief from either the NCCK, the Catholic church or the

---

[131] Interview with Ernest Murimi, Executive Secretary, Justice and Peace Commission of the Catholic Diocese of Nakuru, Nakuru District, June 24, 1993.

[132] Interview with Fr. Peter Elungata, Burnt Forest Catholic Church, Eldoret, Uasin Gishu District, June 29, 1993.

[133] Ibid.

[134] Interview with Moses Ote, NCCK relief coordinator, Nairobi, June 21, 1993.

Kenyan Red Cross. The enormity of the situation and the urgent need for the government to provide relief assistance is underscored by the fact that the NCCK currently spends Kshs 16 million [US $200,000] on food alone *each month* to feed an estimated 200,000 people in ten districts.[135] The government needs to cooperate with these local non-governmental organizations to ensure that victims of the violence are assisted.

---

[135] Interview with Samuel Kobia, NCCK Secretary General, Nairobi, July 13, 1993.

6. GOVERNMENT OBSTRUCTION

Another aspect of the violence has been the government's consistent efforts to attack and obstruct individuals and organizations who have attempted to monitor the violence or assist the victims. In striking contrast to the government's lack of action against those responsible for the violence, it has been quick to mobilize state power to intimidate others from monitoring or reporting on the violence. In addition to the government's suppression of the Kiliku Report, the Speaker of the House has also ensured that any meaningful discussion of the clashes in Parliament is blocked. In April 1993, the Democratic Party (DP) introduced a motion into Parliament calling for the government to take immediate action to stop the clashes. KANU politicians immediately introduced an illegal amendment changing the wording to call for the government to "intensify its efforts to contain the situation."[136] As one opposition politician pointed out, "The government has followed the amendment. The clashes have been 'contained,' but they have not been stopped, even though the government certainly has control over them."[137]

There have also been numerous attacks on the independent press and individual journalists for their coverage of the violence. Prominent environmentalist Wangari Maathai and her colleagues have been harassed since forming an organization called the Tribal Clashes Resettlement Volunteer Service. Church officials have likewise been harassed for their efforts to assist clash victims. "Efforts to organize victims have been stopped by the government because the government fears the conscientization of the people," Executive Secretary of the Catholic Justice and Peace Commission Ernest Murimi pointed out. "Allowing the two sides to get together and to reconcile would make it more difficult for the government to manipulate them in the future."

---

[136] There is a standing order to the effect that an amendment that negates the effect of a motion cannot be introduced in Parliament.

[137] Interview with Martha Njoka, DP MP, Nairobi, June 20, 1993.

ATTACKS ON THE INDEPENDENT PRESS

President Moi has consistently accused the outspoken independent media of being responsible for the ethnic violence through "biased" reporting. In March 1992, the President cautioned the press against sensational reporting, referring to the clashes. The government, concerned about the international repercussions of banning publications outright, is resorting instead to a combination of legal and extra-legal methods to drive its critics out of business.[138] Outspoken magazines, such as *Finance, Society,* and the *Nairobi Law Monthly,* have faced a campaign of threats, arrests, charges, and seizures for covering stories such as the ethnic clashes. The private television station, KTN, ceased its broadcast of local news on February 28, 1993, stating that it had become too expensive. The evening before, the station had led off its evening news program with a story on the opposition FORD-A leader, Kenneth Matiba, giving an ultimatum to the government to stop the clashes.

In February 1993, Njehu Gatabaki, editor of *Finance* magazine was held for nearly a month before being released on sedition charges. *Finance* magazine has consistently covered the clashes, and a number of issues have been confiscated. He was arrested again in June as he prepared to attend the World Conference on Human Rights in Vienna. In April 1993, a group of armed men identifying themselves as police officers broke into the offices of *Finance* magazine, smashed the computers and stabbed the computer manager, David Njau, who was later admitted to hospital suffering from deep cuts in his arms. The attackers stole the artwork for the next issue and a large amount of money intended for salaries and printing costs. *Society* magazine has faced similar attacks. Sedition charges were brought in April 1992 against its editor, Pius Nyamora; they were finally dropped in May 1993. Several issues of the magazine have been illegally confiscated by the government, and in June 1992 the office was petrol-bombed.

On April 30, 1993, the police stormed the printing press of Fotoform Ltd., which was printing a number of outspoken magazines, including *Society, Finance,* and the *Nairobi Law Monthly.* The police

---

[138] *See* Article 19, *Kenya: Continued Attacks on the Independent Press*, Issue 25, May 31, 1993 and Article 19 Bulletin, *Kenya: World Bank Restores Aid Despite Press Crackdown*, August/September 1993, p. 6. All references in this subsection are from these sources unless otherwise noted.

dismantled the machinery and confiscated essential parts from the printer. Fotoform's production manager was taken in for questioning by the police on May 3, 1993, and threatened by the police. A few days later, the company's director, Dominic Martin, was charged with attempting to print a seditious publication. In September 1993, the charges were withdrawn. By that time, Fotoform had suffered five months of lost revenue; as had the publications, which had lost sales and advertising revenues.

In May 1993, security officers impounded 6,000 copies of *Jitegemea* magazine without explanation from its distribution offices and street vendors. The monthly magazine, published by the Presbyterian Church of East Africa (PCEA), had carried a cover story titled, "666, War is War," in which they had criticized KANU leaders, including George Saitoti, Nicholas Biwott, Kipkalia Kones, Paul Chepkok, Sharif Nassir, William ole Ntimama, and Joseph Kamotho, saying that the group, "spells doom for Kenya as a nation." The article discussed the ethnic clashes, drawing parallels to the extermination of Jews during the Second World War.[139]

On August 1, 1993, police raided Colourprint, the printer that had begun to print *Finance* and *Society* after the Fotoform incident. The police seized 20,000 copies of *Finance* magazine and detained the son of one of Colourprint's directors for several hours.

Individual journalists who have reported on the clashes have also come under attack. Cathy Majtenyi, a Canadian journalist doing feature stories on the clashes for the *Daily Nation* newspaper, was attacked by unknown assailants in downtown Nairobi after returning with information from the clash areas on May 22, 1993. Ms. Majtenyi told Africa Watch, "Everywhere I went, I gathered shocking and graphic testimonies of clash violence and evidence that government officials at all levels were involved. I took many pictures and recorded the testimonies of everyone I talked to."[140] At approximately 8:00 P.M. on the night Ms. Majtenyi returned to Nairobi, she disembarked at the bus stop and began to walk to another bus stop to catch her bus home. Feeling nervous, she transferred several notebooks and film canisters from her

---

[139] "Officers Impound Magazine in Raid," *Daily Nation*, May 30, 1993.

[140] Interview with Cathy Majtenyi, Ontario, Canada, September 30, 1993. *See also* "'Nation' Reporter Robbed in City," *Daily Nation*, May 23, 1993.

bag to her pockets and tied her jacket around her waist to ensure that if her bag was snatched for any reason she would still have her information. She noticed three young, well-dressed men behind her.   When she stopped to cross the street in the middle of town near the Hilton Hotel, she was suddenly accosted and held in a chokehold.   In seconds, her glasses were thrown off her face and her bag snatched.   When she checked her pockets, her film and notebooks were gone.   However, her money and passport in her pockets and a pouch were untouched.   A witness to the attack later told Ms. Majtenyi that she had been followed for some time by the men and that, until they attacked her, he had thought that she was with them.   Ms. Majtenyi told Africa Watch

> Whether the incident was a simple robbery or a calculated political move.   I cannot prove for sure. However, I felt that the timing of the attack was too coincidental.   I   had   been   mugged   in   Nairobi approximately five times before. This felt different. The fact that the men were well-dressed and left the most valuable things behind (money, watch, passport, glasses), plus the fact that, later, the telephone calls I made to my contacts to tell them of the robbery kept getting cut off, leads me to believe that it may have not been a simple "tourist" robbery.[141]

---

[141] Ibid.

HARASSMENT OF THE TRIBAL CLASHES
RESETTLEMENT VOLUNTEER SERVICE

The Tribal Clashes Resettlement Volunteer Service is an organization formed in February 1993 by prominent environmentalist Wangari Maathai. On January 15, 1993, Ms. Maathai visited the Burnt Forest area in Uasin Gishu District, along with international and local journalists. Following her return to Nairobi, she announced the creation of an organization called the Tribal Clashes Resettlement Volunteer Service (TCRVS). The government response was to accuse her of inciting the clashes.[142]

The organization put out a number of leaflets urging Kenyans to act to end the violence, including one entitled "Tribal (Political) Clashes . . . Down the Road." The sharply worded leaflet indicted the government, stating,

> The ongoing tribal (political) clashes are politically motivated, well-organized and stage-managed by politicians who have trained and equipped their tribesmen, and probably mercenaries, with sophisticated arrows to kill, destroy, and loot from unprepared and unsuspecting Kenyans.

The leaflet also sketched a five-stage scenario anticipating that the escalating violence could result in the government mobilizing the various security forces which could "unleash untold brutality to civilians especially non-Kalenjins," eventually resulting in a Somalia-type situation.[143]

Ms. Maathai also announced that the organization would be initiating a resettlement program and a reconciliation seminar for clash victims. However, the government immediately mobilized its security and police forces to block off the church where the seminar was scheduled, preventing the victims from gathering. A second and third seminar were organized to take place in the Catholic church in Nakuru in March 1993.

---

[142] "Maathai Stirring Up Hatred," *Kenya Times*, January 31, 1993.

[143] Tribal Clashes Resettlement Volunteer Service, *Tribal (Political) Clashes ....
Down the Road*, April 1992.

However, both seminars faced the same fate as the first one. Regular police, Criminal Investigation Department (CID) officers, local government officials and General Service Unit (GSU)[144] troops surrounded the church compound preventing people from entering. Lawyer James Orengo who tried to attend the second seminar told Africa Watch,

> I arrived at the church, but before I could cross the road
> into the compound, a cordon of about thirty plainclothes
> policemen with four dogs stopped me. I explained that
> I was attending church and they told me that I had no
> business attending church in Nakuru.[145]

Following the second seminar, two men were arrested for distributing seditious leaflets (the TCRVS leaflet) in Nakuru, Eldoret and Thika. One of the members of the organization was held for two weeks without charge after being arrested at a bus stop in possession of a number of the leaflets.[146]

On February 25, 1993, a colleague of Ms. Maathai who had previously been distributing relief and medicine to clash victims was harassed. Mr. John Makanga, a pharmacist, was dragged out of his pharmacy at approximately 9:00 P.M. by approximately twenty hooded police and detained without trial. On the evening of February 25, Mr. Makanga was summoned to the police station for questioning by approximately ten plainclothes policemen who visited the pharmacy, demanding that he accompany them. Mr. Makanga refused, stating that he would to only if accompanied by his lawyer. The police left. Believing that he would be safer at the pharmacy, which is located in the downtown Hilton Hotel, Mr. Makanga stayed in his upstairs office at the

---

[144] The GSU are the paramilitary wing of the police known for their brutality. See Africa Watch, *Taking Liberties* (July 1991), p. 83.

[145] Interview with James Orengo, lawyer, Nairobi, July 12, 1993.

[146] Interview with Nyaguthii Chege, Green Belt Movement, Nairobi, June 19, 1993.

pharmacy.[147] Close to midnight, approximately seventy police surrounded the area and cleared the taxi stand outside the pharmacy. Approximately twenty hooded and gloved policemen then dragged Mr. Makanga out of the pharmacy. Mr. Makanga's lawyer, James Orengo, witnessed the incident. Mr. Orengo told Africa Watch,

> They came upstairs to his office, and then they climbed over the desk and grabbed Makanga by the jacket and hair and started dragging him down the stairs. The office area was too small and the winding staircase too narrow, so the first attempt did not work. Another group came up with guns. Finally, they overpowered Makanga and dragged him head first through the hotel lobby and put him in the boot of a stationwagon car and sped off. We tried to follow, but lost track. We didn't know where Makanga was for two days until he appeared in court.[148]

Mr. Makanga was held without charge over the weekend at the nearby remand center; however, his whereabouts during that time were unknown to his lawyer and family. When Mr. Makanga was brought into court under charges of distributing seditious publications, he immediately requested that a doctor examine him. He had been severely beaten and denied food for three days. The magistrate, Babu Achieng, denied bail, but ordered medical treatment for Mr. Makanga. However, the following day he had still not seen a doctor, and the court was forced to order the police to admit Mr. Makanga into Nairobi Hospital at his own cost. Mr. Makanga stayed in the hospital for two weeks before being released on bail. The charges were dropped eventually.

In June 1993, at the Vienna World Conference on Human Rights, a photo exhibition on the ethnic clashes mounted by Maathai was vandalized by a delegation of "traditional Maasais."[149] The delegation

---

[147] Ibid.

[148] Interview with James Orengo, lawyer, Nairobi, July 12, 1993.

[149] Interview with Gitobu Imanyara, *Nairobi Law Monthly* editor, Boston, USA, August, 1993 and "Maathai's Vienna Stand Raided," *Daily Nation*, June 20, 1993.

of Maasais, led by Local Government Minister William ole Ntimama, had been sponsored by the government to represent Kenya's indigenous peoples. Copies of the Kiliku Report and the NEMU report on the violence were also stolen from the stand.

HARASSMENT OF CHURCH RELIEF WORKERS

Local government authorities have consistently harassed church officials who have permitted victims to stay on church property. In Burnt Forest, the local Catholic priest, Fr. Peter Elungata, was summoned to the local police station for questioning by the district officer, after he had allowed approximately 15,000 people (predominantly Kikuyu, Luhya and Turkana) to stay on his church compound.[150]   Moses Ote, NCCK Relief Coordinator, has faced harassment several times while organizing food distribution in the clash areas.   In Bungoma District, he was detained overnight on November 18, 1992, for "instigating" the clashes. On another occasion at Kapkateny, Bungoma District, he was arrested for protesting the forced dispersal of displaced victims by the district commissioner.   In April 1993, the district officer in Kimilili, Bungoma District, tried to prevent the NCCK from distributing food to clash victims on the grounds that the NCCK food relief program was the reason why clash victims were not returning to their homes.[151]   He told NCCK officials that his instructions were from the district commissioner. The Executive Secretary of the Catholic Justice and Peace Commission for Nakuru, Ernest Murimi, was summoned to the police station in May 1993 for his work with clash victims in the Nakuru area. Presbyterian Minister Rev. Samuel Macharia Muchuga was summoned to the police station twice in 1992 to "explain" his sermons to the police.

The harassment at the local levels has been accompanied by excoriating attacks by President Moi on the churches. In February 1993, President Moi accused the NCCK of "exploiting the plight of displaced clash victims to solicit funds from overseas for their own use." He also

---

[150] Interview with Fr. Peter Elungata, Burnt Forest Catholic church, Eldoret, Uasin Gishu District, June 29, 1993.

[151] Interview with Salvation Army Captain, Kimilili, Bungoma District, July 3, 1993.

said that many of the victims were "squatters seeking free meals and clothes."[152]

The government has not hesitated to cancel the work permits of expatriate priests who have been assisting clash victims. To date, four Catholic priests have had their work permits withdrawn. Fr. Robert Cavanaugh, who had assisted victims from the Kamwaura area of Molo, Nakuru District, was deported from Kenya in July 1992.[153] Fr. Oliver Ryan, an expatriate priest at Marigat Parish whose work permit was valid until 1996, received a letter from Principal Immigration Officer J.Z. Onduko on May 6, 1993, ordering him to leave the country within a week. The month before, Fr. Ryan had signed a letter as part of the Marigat Parish Justice and Peace Committee, complaining to the Marigat district officer, Mr. Cheruiyot (a Kalenjin), that non-Kalenjin people at Marigat were being intimidated.[154] A High Court order was obtained to stay the execution of the deportation order pending the hearing of the case showing that Fr. Ryan had not contravened the Immigration Act.[155]

---

[152] "Clashes: Moi Tells of NCCK's Role," *Daily Nation*, February 21, 1993.

[153] NEMU, *Courting Disaster*, (April 29, 1993), p. 8.

[154] "Priest Ordered to Quit," *Daily Nation*, May 19, 1993.

[155] "High Court Halts Priest's Deportation," *Daily Nation*, May 20, 1993.

7. GOVERNMENT HARASSMENT OF CLASH VICTIMS

The government's lack of concern has been underscored by its callous treatment of clash victims who congregate in large numbers at church compounds or near-by abandoned buildings seeking refuge. Hundreds of thousands of clash victims are housed with relatives or in makeshift camps and market centers because of valid fears of recurring violence if they return to their land. Some have lived this way for over a year. Often, individuals attempting to return to their land have faced intimidation or even death from Kalenjin warriors. These isolated incidents send a strong message to dissuade others from returning. Since most of the dispossessed victims are farmers who, having lost their land, are now unable to support themselves and their families, they remain in the camps dependent on food relief from the churches.

Local government authorities continually downplay the magnitude of the violence, or disperse victims who congregate in large numbers. "A lot depends on the local DC [district commissioner] and whether they want to help people," a diplomat told Africa Watch. "Some are very partisan. The worst DCs are Paul Langat of Uasin Gishu and Ben Magoga of Trans Nzoia."[156] In Bungoma District, Africa Watch visited Kapkateny and Namwela camps where approximately a hundred clash victims were being housed in make-shift housing or abandoned buildings. Yet, when asked about the situation, a Bungoma district officer denied the existence of the camps and told Africa Watch that the clashes "were a problem a year ago, but now we don't have that problem anymore."[157]

To ensure that large gatherings of clash victims are not easily visible to visiting human rights groups, the media, or foreign diplomats, local government officials disperse camps without any consideration of where these victims will go. One method that is frequently used by local government officials is to announce to the victims, despite evidence to the contrary, that it is safe to return to their land. Another method that local

---

[156] Interview with diplomat (name withheld by request), Nairobi, June 18, 1993.

[157] Interview with district officer, Bungoma, Bungoma District, July 5, 1993.

government officials have used when victims have fled to church compounds is to accuse church officials of incitement for allowing people to stay and of holding illegal meetings on their compound.[158] Where victims do not leave voluntarily, local government officials, with the assistance of the police, forcibly disperse camps of displaced people without providing adequate assistance or security to permit them to return to their land.

Destitute and unable to return to their land, clash victims who have been dispersed are at the mercy of the government authorities. Most leave the camp that they are evicted from and settle on near by land. They rebuild their makeshift shelters, hoping not to be forced to flee yet again.

THE CASE OF ENDEBESS CAMP

On June 3, 1993, government authorities cleared a camp of displaced Luhyas and Tesos at Endebess in Trans Nzoia district. The camp residents had fled there on December 26, 1991, after approximately 400 Kalenjins (Sabaot and Sebei), armed with bows and arrows and wearing red shirts and shorts with clay smeared on their faces, attacked their cooperative farm--Mango farm.[159]

The local police were notified of the attack by the victims of the violence and were given the names of some of the Kalenjin attackers, who were recognized. Witnesses verify that although some attackers were arrested, they were released unconditionally the following day. Other clash victims told Africa Watch that although they had registered complaints with the police, identifying some of the Kalenjin warriors, the attackers were not arrested. Some of the Kalenjins responsible for the violence continue to occupy Mango farm without any sanction. One young Luhya man told Africa Watch that he could identify some of the Kalenjin attackers who had driven him off his land, including eight by the

---

[158] Although there is no legal basis to prosecute such charges, church officials have subsequently made arrangements to find rentals to house victims to avoid the harassment from government authorities. Interview with Fr. Peter Elungata, Burnt Forest Catholic church, Eldoret, Uasin Gishu District, June 29, 1993.

[159] Interview with Luhya clash victim, Bidii farm, Trans Nzoia district, June 30, 1993.

names of Kapkaset, Andrei, Kamron, Peter Kisiero, Charles Masai, Joseph Salare, John Kibisi, and Masai Kisasia. He noted that they continued to live at Mango farm.[160]

Initially, approximately 8,000 people sought refuge on the plot of public land at Endebess. Conditions at the camp were appalling. Makeshift shelters of stick and plastic sheeting provided the only cover against the rain. No government assistance was forthcoming, and the only food relief was provided by the churches. The displaced elders at Endebess camp organized an elementary school run by volunteers to ensure that the 1,800 displaced children could continue their education. Over time, the number of victims at the Endebess camp decreased to approximately 2,000 as the remainder found housing elsewhere. In May 1993, the authorities claimed that it had become safe for the victims to return to the land, despite evidence to the contrary.

Since the attack on December 26, 1991, Kalenjins have been occupying Mango farm and have gone so far as to rename it Mosop farm, a Kalenjin name. Some Endebess camp residents who attempted to resettle on their land at Mango farm were attacked, which discouraged others from returning.[161] Africa Watch spoke to Sabaot Kalenjins near Mango farm who told Africa Watch that they did not know why the fighting started and they had also suffered. When asked if they owned the land, they claimed that they had bought it. They also said that others were welcome to farm on the land.[162]

On May 26, 1993, local government authorities, including the chief, who are predominantly Kalenjin, informed the Endebess camp residents that the land was a County Council plot and that they had to leave by June 3, 1993. "I was there," a church official told Africa Watch, "The local authorities threatened them the day before they were supposed to leave. When we intervened with the local district commissioner, he told us that so many people had visited the camp, including the UN and a European Community delegation, that the government was

---

[160] Interview with Luhya clash victim, Bidii farm, June 30, 1993.

[161] Interview with Luhya clash victim, Bidii farm, June 30, 1993.

[162] Interview with Kalenjin (Sabaot) men, Quintin farm, Trans Nzoia District, June 30, 1993.

embarrassed and did not want the camp there any more."[163] The local chief also told residents that they had to leave the camp to end the visits by foreigners who took pictures of them, thereby giving Kenya a bad name.

The government did not provide any alternative accommodation or any assistance to the camp residents to assist them with relocating. Once they were hounded from Endebess camp, the camp residents had nowhere else to go except to neighboring farms including Bidii, Khalwenge, Matisi, and Bikeke farms. Africa Watch visited Bidii farm, a privately owned farm, to which approximately one hundred of the former Endebess camp residents had relocated. Tiny makeshift shelters on bare earth with up to fifteen or more people sleeping in each provided no protection from the rain. The owner of Bidii farm, Khaemba Sikenga, who had also been the treasurer of the cooperative that was buying Mango farm, protested the appearance of the displaced on his farm and asked the district commissioner to evict them. Pending their eviction, he made each person pay him Kshs. 50 [US $0.75] for the use of a near-by tap for water--an exorbitant amount for the displaced families. To date, only the NCCK has provided victims with material and food assistance.

Many of the victims believe that they have lost their land permanently. They had been purchasing the land jointly as a cooperative, making payments over a long period of time. By the time they were forced off their land, they had paid millions of shillings towards owning the land, but had not completed their payments. The Mango farm residents have not only lost possession of their land, but also believe that they have lost the money that they had invested toward owning it.

Other camps have also faced similar treatment from the government. In Kapkateny in Bungoma District, the government is threatening to evict approximately one hundred Luhya victims who have taken refuge in an unused government-owned maize warehouse. The victims have been denied permission to build a shelter nearby to reduce the congestion.[164]

---

[163] Interview with Ephraim Kiragu, NCCK outreach director, Nairobi, June 18, 1993.

[164] Ibid.

EFFECTS OF THE VIOLENCE

8. IMPLICATIONS OF THE VIOLENCE

The total impact of the violence in Kenya is literally incalculable. Certainly, over 1,500 have been killed and hundreds of thousands displaced. The implications of the violence, however, go far beyond the figures. The clashes have already had lasting effects that will alter Kenya's political and economic development for many years, even if the violence were to end today.

Much of the destruction and destabilization has worked to the political and economic advantage of President Moi and his inner circle. Before the election, the violence disrupted voter registration in communities that predominantly supported the opposition. The violence has also allowed the government to punish those ethnic groups who voted against KANU in the election. Since the election, the violence has allowed the Kalenjin community to capitalize on the insecurity to occupy or buy land at low prices from destitute non-Kalenjins who cannot return to their land. Patterns of land ownership in the Rift Valley are being permanently altered, with significant political implications for consolidating KANU rule in the future. The "ethnic" violence has also created the potential for an explosive situation. A rapidly growing population of dispossessed Kenyans, the majority of whom are children, have no stake in the nation's future. These effects of the violence are discussed in detail below.

VOTER REGISTRATION DISRUPTED BEFORE THE ELECTION

The outbreak of the violence during the voter registration period significantly affected the registration totals in the clash areas. The international Commonwealth monitoring team that observed the election estimated that as many as 1.5 million eligible voters had not been

John G. Watson

Translation and Reproduction Section
Conference Services

UNITED NATIONS ENVIRONMENT PROGRAMME

P.O. Box 30552 (Off.)
P.O. Box 47074 (Pvt.)
NAIROBI
Kenya.

Telephone: 623347, 621234
Fax: (2542) 226886, 228890
Telex: 22068 UNEP KE

registered to vote.[165] Hundreds from the clash areas were unable to register because the violence prevented them from returning to their home areas. It is likely that the majority of this group would have supported the political opposition had they been able to cast their vote.

A GROWING NUMBER OF DEAD AND DISPLACED

The most apparent effect of the violence has been the large number of casualties and the growing number of formerly self-sufficient farmers who have been dispossessed of their land, perhaps permanently. Africa Watch estimates that over 1,500 people have died in the clashes and that approximately 300,000 people are displaced.

The number of dead and displaced persons has been difficult to document accurately. The Kiliku Report in September 1992 estimated the number of dead at 800. A year later, the figure has certainly doubled. "In many places, the count of the dead was inaccurate," a journalist told Africa Watch. "Many bodies killed in forest areas were eaten by animals and those were not counted. In other cases, people are still counted as 'missing.' I know one person in Londiani who lost a cousin last year, but his body has never been found."

The count of the displaced has been equally difficult to ascertain. Africa Watch found in many places that the count of displaced persons cited included only the adults, ignoring large numbers of displaced children. Many victims have not been identified by the government or by those distributing relief, either because they are living in the homes of friends and relatives or because they have not yet come to the attention of the authorities. Periodically, hundreds of victims are "discovered" whose situation was previously unknown. A decentralized relief distribution system operated by numerous organizations has also made it difficult to verify an overall number. Also, with the violence continuing, the figures are constantly rising.

The most reliable source for the number of displaced comes from NCCK food distribution figures. In January 1993, the NCCK reported

---

[165] Commonwealth Secretariat, *The Presidential, Parliamentary and Civic Elections in Kenya,* The Report of the Commonwealth Observer Group, December 29, 1992, p. (viii).

that is was feeding approximately 170,000 people each month.[166] By July 1993, this figure had risen to over 200,000. The Catholic church in Nakuru District alone is assisting approximately 40,000 victims. Additional displaced victims are being assisted by the Kenya Red Cross, making the total number even higher. The fact that the violence is continuing and that most victims are unable to return to their land ensures that this figure will continue to rise.

The NCCK Eldoret District Office has instituted a registration system that has accurately documented the number of displaced persons receiving food assistance in the Eldoret area in Uasin Gishu. By July 1993, in that *one* District, there were 120,000 *registered and documented* displaced persons, the majority of whom were children, receiving food relief each month.[167] Of the group, a quarter were Kalenjin while the majority were Kikuyu, Luhya, and Luo. The NCCK pastor in the area, Samson Khalwale, told Africa Watch that they were still discovering people who were just finding out that relief was available and were asking for help. These figures do not address assistance being given to other displaced people in the district by the Catholic church, the Kenya Red Cross, Catholic Relief Services, the Church Province of Kenya, Action Aid and other non-governmental organizations. The NCCK is beginning to expand its registration system to the other affected Districts, which will further confirm the estimated figures of over 200,000; efforts are underway to coordinate the distribution of food by various organizations.

---

[166] The breakdown for the figures is: Bungoma District, 36,436; Uasin Gishu District, 54,094; Trans Nzoia District, 14,152; Nakuru District, over 51,000; Kisumu District, 14,000. NCCK, *Update on Politicised Land Clashes*, January 1993. he Christian Reformed World Relief Committee estimated a displaced count of 41,000 in Bungoma District by April 1993. Christian Reformed World Relief Committee, *Report on Displaced Persons in Bungoma District*, June 14, 1993.

[167] According to this system, a form is completed for each family, noting the number of children and whether one or both parents are with the children. Each family is issued a blue, numbered registration card which is marked each time they receive food from the NCCK. The plot number of the land that the displaced have come from is also noted to verify the situation. The NCCK had registered 14,672 families by July 1993 and estimated that there were an average of seven children per family. Interview with Pastor Samson Khalwale, NCCK District Office, Eldoret, Uasin Gishu District, June 29, 1993.

In May 1993, a United Nations Development Program (UNDP) Disaster Management Team mission estimated the number of displaced at 114,136; however, this figure does not even cover the number of NCCK registered displaced persons receiving assistance in Uasin Gishu.[168] Another UNDP document assessing the situation of displaced persons in the Horn of Africa quotes a more accurate figure of 223,700, attributing it to the NCCK.[169] On October 26, 1993, the Kenyan government and UNDP released a joint programme document on the clashes placing the number of displaced persons in April 1993 at 255,426.[170]

Despite the joint Kenya government-UNDP report, the official figures for the dead and displaced cited by the government is significantly lower than all other estimates (including its own in the joint report with UNDP). In May 1993, a Minister of State in the Office of the President released a statement in Parliament, claiming that the violence between October 1991 and December 1992 had claimed 365 lives and had displaced 7,113 persons. The Office of the President gave the ethnic breakdown for the dead up to December 1992 as 102 Kikuyus, eighty-seven Kalenjins, sixty-nine Luhyas, forty-four Kisiis, thirty Luos, twelve Maasais, ten Somalis, six Turkanas, four Tesos, and one Arab. The

---

[168] The UNDP team obtained a figure of 89,136 from the areas it visited; Endebess, Sanoti, Trans Nzoia, Kimilili, Kapkateny, Sirisia, Uasin Gishu, Molo/Elburgon and Narok. It estimated that a further 25,000 were taking refuge in other areas such as Kisumu, Kisii, Bungoma, Kericho, Kakamega, Nandi and most recently, Lakipia. UN Disaster Management Team, *Mission to the Affected Areas of Western Kenya affected by the Ethnic Clashes*, May 1993, p. 3-4.

[169] UNDP, *Displaced Populations in the Horn of Africa*, undated, p. 10.

[170] The breakdown of the figures by District is as follows: Bungoma, 21,100; Busia, 1,800; Elgon, 14, 375; Kakamega, unknown; Vihiga, unknown; Kisumu, 8,975; Nyamira 750; Kisii, 2,300; Kuria, unknown; Turkana, 16,625; Trans Nzoia, 18,525; Elgeyo-Marakwet, 22,300; Uasin Gishu, 82,000; Nandi, 17,850; Kericho, 6,550; Bomet, unknown; Narok, 900; Nakuru, 40, 700; Laikipia, 600. UNDP Draft Report "The Internal Displaced Population in Western, Nyanza and Rift Valley Provinces: A Needs Assessment and Rehabilitation Programme," prepared by John R. Rogge, April 28, 1993 as reported in Government of Kenya/UNDP *Programme Document: Programme for Displaced Persons*, Inter-agency joint programming, October 26, 1993, p.8.

government's ethnic breakdown of the displaced population during the same period was 2,382 Luhyas, 1,971 Kikuyus, 1,720 Kalenjins, 403 Luos, 354 Kisiis, 259 Tesos, and twenty-five Kambas.[171]   Mr. Kalweo, who read out the figures, dismissed all other figures as untrue. Attorney-General Amos Wako updated the figures in a meeting with Africa Watch in July 1993, stating that there had been twenty-nine more deaths and sixty-five more displaced in 1993, noting that "of course, these figures are in dispute."[172]

There was an immediate public uproar in response to the government's understatement of the effects of the violence. Opposition politicians rejected the figures as gross underestimates and some pointed out that in their own individual constituencies the figures were larger than the government's overall count.   A number of opposition parliamentarians cited the Kiliku Report which had placed the figures at 799 dead and 54,000 displaced between October 1991 and September 1992. MP for Gichugu, Martha Karua, who had submitted the question to the government, responded to the Minister of State by saying,

> Is the Minister not deliberately misleading the House . . . If truly the displaced persons are at 7,113, they ought to have benefitted to the tune of Kshs. 100,000 [US $1,250] each from the Kshs. 10 million that the government set aside for them. That is not the case and it is clear that this answer is false. Can the Minister respond?[173]

However, Deputy Speaker of the House Bonaya Godana overruled further supplementary questions and refused to allow the debate to continue.

---

[171] "Clashes 'claimed 365'," *Standard*, May 6, 1993 and "Only 365 Killed in Clashes - Govt," *Daily Nation*, May 6, 1993. The government figures given distinguish between the number of Kalenjins and Sabaots arrested. Since the Sabaot are Kalenjin, Africa Watch has joined the two numbers.

[172] Interview with Amos Wako, Attorney-General, Nairobi, July 12, 1993.

[173] Parliamentary Transcript, A.2. Question 174, Casualties of Ethnic Clashes, May 5, 1993.

The government's blatant misrepresentation of the situation prompted a newspaper editorial the following day to state, "[f]or as long as Government Ministers continue handing out distortions, half-truths, and outright lies, for that long will they feed on the suspicion of illegitimacy which lingers in the minds of most people."[174] The NCCK issued a press statement rejecting the government's figures as "untrue, baseless and malicious" as did the Catholic church, both citing the total for the displaced as over 100,000."[175]

---

[174] "Clashes: Faulty Maths or Deliberate Distortion?" *Daily Nation*, May 7, 1993, p. 6.

[175] "NCCK, Press Statement," *Target*, May 20, 1993, p. 11 and "'Nation' Report Riles Ntimama," *Daily Nation*, May 7, 1993.

ALTERING LAND OWNERSHIP IN RIFT VALLEY PROVINCE

A long-term effect of the violence is the fact that land ownership patterns in Rift Valley Province are being permanently altered to reduce the numbers of non-Kalenjin land-holders in the Province. Not surprisingly, many non-Kalenjins chased off their land are moving out. Correspondingly, Kalenjins are moving in--either by illegally occupying land or buying it. Opposition politician and lawyer, Martha Karua, told Africa Watch,

> at first, the attacks consisted of chasing people off the land and then looting. Now, victims are so scared that they are selling land at throwaway prices. These land transfers are being registered and soon people will not be able to go back because it won't be their land anymore.[176]

The increased possession of land by Kalenjins in the Rift Valley benefits the Moi government by allowing it to claim that it is satisfying Kalenjin sentiments that the government deserves continued political support for getting "their" land back and increasing their economic wealth.

The continuing intimidation coupled with the repeated calls for a *majimbo* (regional) system by KANU politicians has led to the widespread perception on the part of non-Kalenjins that the government will never allow them to return to their land. These fears are well-founded. A Kalenjin told Africa Watch that his community in the Nakuru area had agreed that "they were unwilling to let any Kikuyu return to the Olenguruone area or to allow other Kikuyus to buy the land. If by chance a Kikuyu did manage to buy land there, they would not allow the Kikuyu to stay on the land. They feel that they have been put down by the Kikuyu for too long."[177]

The suspicions by non-Kalenjins that they will not get their land back are further fueled by the fact that many of those kept from their land report that they have been offered sums significantly below market

---

[176] Interview with Martha Karua, DP MP, Nairobi, June 20, 1993.

[177] Interview with Kalenjin man, Nakuru, Nakuru District, June 24, 1993.

value for their farms. Those that refuse to sell are given warnings by their Kalenjin neighbors, that a time will come when they will not only have to sell, but will have to accept the price given to them by Kalenjins.[178]

In Uasin Gishu District, Kikuyu clash victims from Rukuini, Kamunyu, Kodoo, and Rironi have reported being approached by groups of people seeking to buy their land with offers significantly below market value. They claimed that those who were approaching them were offering Kshs. 20,000 [US $250] because "that is the amount that has been agreed upon by buyers regarding the purchase of all farms owned by non-Kalenjins in the Rift Valley." The market price for an acre of land in that area before the clashes was between Kshs 80,000-100,000 [US $1,000-1,250]. Local government administrators have admitted that there have been increased land sales in the area, but have denied that there has been any coercion.[179]

At Sirisia, Bungoma District, an elderly Luhya man who owned a twenty-five acre plot told Africa Watch that he had been offered Kshs. 25,000 [US $312] for his land. The market price for that land before the violence would have been Kshs. 750,000 [US $9,375]. The old man had fled his land in April 1992 along with other Luhyas from the area after being attacked by approximately one hundred Kalenjins, dressed in skins and shorts with clay on their faces, who burned and looted the Luhyas' homes. Since that time, it has not been safe enough to return. When he had tried, he heard gunshots and fled. A teacher, Francis Juma na Mayengo, who had moved into the old man's house to take care of it for him was found hacked to death on March 30, 1993. The GSU security officials who visited the site did nothing more than pick up the body.[180] Others from the area who have tried to return have been similarly killed. One victim told Africa Watch, that "on April 17, 1993, seven people returned to their land with two askaris [guards]. As they

---

[178] "Kenya Cleansed," *BBC Focus on Africa*, Vol. 4, No. 3, July-September 1993, p. 18.

[179] "Victims 'Asked to Sell their Farms,'" *Daily Nation*, May 14, 1993 and "Biwott Men Target Clash Victims' Land," *The People*, June 27,-July 3, 1993.

[180] Interview with elderly Luhya man, Sirisia, Bungoma District, July 1, 1993.

crossed the Tisi river, they heard gunshots. One askari, John Nyongeza, was shot in the chest."[181]

Other non-Kalenjins have exchanged land with people who are willing to take their plot in return for land in another province. In some areas, local Kalenjin authorities have explicitly instructed clash victims to exchange their land with Kalenjins from outside the Rift Valley. In Tapsagoi, a local Kalenjin chief threatened renewed violence unless the non-Kalenjins, who had fled their land after an attack by Kalenjins, exchanged it with Kalenjins, in violation of the Land Control Board rules.[182] In the Burnt Forest area, Uasin Gishu District, Kikuyus who have attempted to return to their land after being chased off by Kalenjin warriors in December 1992 have found their rebuilt houses destroyed. Others have found the door to their rebuilt home removed or fences around their plot of land taken down. "These are messages to us," a Kikuyu victim told Africa Watch. "So far three people have swapped their land with Kalenjins because they know that they will not be allowed to go back."[183]

Government officials have also not hesitated to misuse their legal authority to expropriate land under the guise of exercising "eminent domain," which allows the government to take over land for the public interest under limited circumstances. In September 1993, the Minister for Local Government, William ole Ntimama, a Maasai who has led the *majimbo* calls, declared an area in his District a trust land for the Narok County Council. His action was confirmed and supported by Minister for Environment and Natural Resources John Sambu, who told residents of the forty-four square kilometer area that they had to move, because the land would soon be gazetted as a protected area. Not coincidentally, the area's 15,600 inhabitants are predominantly Kikuyu. Most of the residents of the area had bought the land from Maasai leaders in the 1960s. They believe that they are being harassed for not having

---

[181] Interview with Luhya clash victim, Sirisia, Bungoma District, July 1, 1993.

[182] "Kenya Cleansed," *BBC Focus on Africa*, Vol. 4, No. 3, July-September 1993, p. 17-18.

[183] Interview with Kikuyu clash victim, Laingushe camp, Burnt Forest, Uasin Gishu District, June 29, 1993.

supported KANU in the election.[184]   In May 1993 in Nakuru, the police demolished the kiosks of street hawkers who had licences to sell their wares. All the vendors who lost their livelihood were Kikuyu. To date, the vendors have not been able to return to the area. Local government authorities have assigned them another area which is out of town and not near the commercial traffic.[185]

In a meeting with Attorney-General Amos Wako, Africa Watch inquired as to whether his office was taking steps to investigate the persistent reports of land sales effected under duress and to nullify such land transfers. Mr. Wako told Africa Watch that "if there is any land that is being sold this way, there is the general law and they can follow it to nullify a contract." Many Kenyan lawyers believe that this inaction on the part of the government is deliberate. They point out that many of the displaced landholders are poor and unaware of their legal rights, making it unlikely that such transfers will ever be challenged unless the government takes steps to protect these people. "To ignore the extra-ordinary situation and to act as though such land transfers are just routine contract disputes," lawyer Chiuri Ngugi told Africa Watch, "is an abrogation of the government's responsibility to acknowledge the illegal nature of these land transfers."[186]

CONSOLIDATING KALENJIN AND KANU POLITICAL POWER

The clashes, while appearing to be senseless violence with no political motive, have, in fact, benefitted the government politically. The government has been able to polarize ethnic sentiments to ensure that the Kalenjin community has no choice but to support the Moi government. Moreover, the government has used the violence to reward and empower the Kalenjin community by allowing its members to occupy or buy land illegally in the Rift Valley Province, the most fertile farmland in the country. Correspondingly, the ethnic polarization and violence

---

[184] "Residents 'Won't Leave Narok'," *Daily Nation*, October 1, 1993, p. 4.

[185] Interview with Ernest Murimi, executive secretary, Justice and Peace Commission, Catholic Diocese of Nakuru, Nakuru District, June 24, 1993.

[186] Interview with Chiuri Ngugi, Executive Director, Legal Education and Aid Program, Nairobi, July 25, 1993.

have served to destabilize areas from which the political opposition would have been able to garner considerable support and to punish ethnic groups who have supported the political opposition.

The transformation of the Rift Valley Province into a Kalenjin land-owning area also has significant political implications. Since the Rift Valley Province is allocated the largest number of seats in Parliament (44 of 188), the KANU government is making long-term political gains for a future election by consolidating Kalenjin political hegemony. If the government decides to implement a *majimbo* system in the future, the stage will be set. Accusations of ethnic cleansing in the Rift Valley are not unwarranted.

CHILDREN: A LOST GENERATION

Kenya is a country with an annual growth rate of over four percent, one of the highest in the world. The average Kenyan woman has between six to eight children; over half the population is under fifteen years of age. Accordingly, children have suffered disproportionally in the clashes. Africa Watch found that in most of the camps visited, the number of children was double that of the adults. As a result of the crowded camp conditions, many of these children are showing signs of infectious diseases such as respiratory problems and tuberculosis as well as scabies and malnutrition.[187]

The violence has deeply affected the children. Many of the children have witnessed their family members being killed and their houses burned down. In some cases, they have themselves suffered injuries from an attack. These children have acquired a keen awareness of their ethnicity and that of their attackers. Prior to the clashes, children of all ethnic groups would play with each other. Now, former friends from different ethnic groups have become sworn enemies. Reports of children displaying aggressive behavior or bringing knives to school have been reported by teachers even outside the clash areas.[188]   Many

---

[187] Interview with Dr. Ling Kituyi, Nairobi, June 26, 1993.

[188] "The Lost Generation," *Daily Nation*, May 29, 1993, p. 11. See also The African Network for the Prevention and Protection against Child Abuse and Neglect (ANPPCAN), "The Effects of Tribal Clashes on Children," *Childwatch*, No. 9, August 1992, p. 6.

children are also suffering nightmares from the violence they have witnessed.

In some areas, the schools are overcrowded as a result of trying to accommodate the large influx of displaced children. Many schools that previously included students of all ethnicities now have students from only one ethnicity. In addition, the education of the majority of displaced children has been disrupted or terminated. The clashes have also prevented secondary school graduates from continuing for higher diplomas because of financial problems. In Trans Nzoia District, the NCCK estimates that over 10,000 children have been displaced and are no longer in school. A similar number are out of school in Bungoma District. In Uasin Gishu District, it is estimated that over 5,000 children are no longer in school as a result of the violence.[189] In Molo, Nakuru District, some fifty-five primary schools catering to over 16,000 children did not reopen in September 1993 because of the violence.[190]

The local primary school at Owiro farm in Nandi District, which used to have 400 predominantly Luo pupils had managed to get back 200 just before a second attack by Kalenjins in March 1992. Now, there are only forty students at the school and the number of teachers has shrunk from eleven to four. The local headmaster told Africa Watch that they lost all their textbooks in the attack, "the pupils do not have uniforms and are hungry all the time and often sick because of their living conditions. They don't study well because they are hungry."[191] In Kapkateny, Bungoma District, the local headmistress of the Kapkateny Primary School told Africa Watch that they had 234 pupils who had been clash victims. "Sometimes the children have to leave school to go look for food because they are always hungry," she observed. "They also often get malaria and are sick."

In cases where parents and volunteers have attempted to create makeshift schools for the displaced children in the camps, the local government authorities have consistently closed down the schools,

---

[189] Interview with Moses Ote, NCCK relief coordinator, Webuye, Bungoma District, June 29, 1993.

[190] "Violence: 55 Schools 'May Not Reopen'," *Daily Nation*, September 2, 1993.

[191] Interview with George Opondo, headmaster, Owiro farm Primary School, Nandi District, July 2, 1993. See p. 51.

depriving the children of any formal educational opportunity whatsoever. A school for 500 children that was started in February 1993 in Trans Nzoia District by Endebess camp residents was quickly shut by local government authorities, who also prohibited the camp's children from attending the local school.[192] In Kapkateny, Bungoma District, the camp residents attempted to establish two schools for 150 children, one at a Pentecostal church and another nearby, but the government closed them both down in March 1993. The Divisional Educational Office, Charles Kaibei, notified the camp residents that the schools had no authority under the Education Act, stating that he did "not like to see a school by [the] name Refugee Camp," and that the children "will in any case be moving to their respective home schools."[193]

A similar story was told to Africa Watch at Namwela camp also in Bungoma District. Teachers, also displaced, had organized a school for ninety-six children in the camp in September 1992. It was closed in May 1993 by the local government officials who told the camp residents that they should go back to their homes and start a school there. The district officer also told the camp residents that he was aware that it was not safe to go back, but that he had been ordered by the government to shut the school down.[194] Teachers pointed out to Africa Watch that their skills were being wasted and even Kalenjin children in some areas who were not displaced were not being taught because teachers have also been displaced. While government concerns about school conditions and academic curriculum in general are valid, the government's unwillingness to recognize that refugee schools are better than none is unnecessarily multiplying the harmful effects on children.

Government officials have been callous in their response to the dire situation. Instead of making educational arrangements to accommodate the hundreds of displaced children, Permanent Secretary

---

[192] "The Lost Generation," *Daily Nation*, May 29, 1993, p. 11.

[193] Interview with Nereah Nabalayo, Headmistress Kapkateny Primary School, Kapkateny, Bungoma District, July 1, 1993, and letter from Charles W. Kaibei, Divisional Education Officer, Kopsiro Division, Chwele to the Headmistress, Kapkateny CPK School (ref. KPS/ST/9/Vol. 1/6), March 15, 1993.

[194] Interview with Luhya teacher, Namwela camp, Namwela, Bungoma District, July 3, 1993.

for Education Benjamin Kipkulei (a Kalenjin) accused parents of not sending their children to their schools for "political gain." He was quoted as saying that all was safe in the clash areas and that the only reason that the displaced families did not return to their homes was because they received "benefits, such as a raised income and sympathy from leaders." In contradiction to the testimonies of teachers, relief workers and parents heard by Africa Watch, Mr. Kipkulei also stated that "by and large, children are going to school."[195]

DESTRUCTION OF COMMUNITIES

The violence has disrupted and destroyed hundreds of communities across the country. Even two years after an attack took place, residents still feel the effects. Distrust between the ethnic groups remains high and the charred remains of buildings are constant reminders of the violence and the possibility of renewed violence. "It is going to take communities at least ten years to get back to where they were before the violence," estimated Ernest Murimi of the Catholic Justice and Peace Commission in Nakuru.[196]

Owiro Farm in Songhor, Nandi District, was one of the first farms affected by the clashes in late 1991. Since that time, the farm has been attacked a second time, and to date its residents are still scared to walk alone on the farm. Owiro Farm exemplifies how the effects of the violence on a community far outlast the event itself. A 2,600-acre plot formerly owned by the Governor of Kenya during the colonial period was bought as a cooperative by 4,000 Luos in 1970. The Kalenjin warriors that attacked in November 1991 completely destroyed the farm, burning the houses and stealing the cattle before leaving. A Luo woman who witnessed the attack described to Africa Watch how the Kalenjins attacked the farm unprovoked at night and set fire to the houses on the farm. "I woke up," she explained, "and I could hear the Kalenjins shouting in the dark 'Luos, you must move.'"[197]

---

[195] "Victims Will Suffer Mentally Forever," *Daily Nation*, May 29, 1993, p. 11.

[196] Interview with Ernest Murimi, Executive Secretary, Justice and Peace Commission, Catholic Diocese of Nakuru, Nakuru District, June 24, 1993.

[197] Interview with Luo clash victim, Owiro farm, Nandi District, July 2, 1993.

When the Parliamentary Select Committee visited the site eight months later, they noted that "[t]he damage effected on Owiro farm was so excruciating that when the Committee visited it on July 6, 1992, there was evidently not a single person in sight."[198] In March 1992, just as life was beginning to return to normal, Owiro farm was attacked for a second time. A Luo resident of the farm told Africa Watch, "in March 1992, they came back and finished the job, just when people were coming back to plant their land. Immediately, people fled [again] and rented houses at the market center."[199]

When Africa Watch visited the farm in July 1993, the destruction was still evident over a year later. The farm is still unsettled. Although approximately one hundred families have returned, much of the land remains uncultivated. People are living in makeshift thatch huts or shelters made of plastic sheeting in place of their houses that were destroyed. The market which used to take place weekly has not been restarted. The reluctance of families to return is further reinforced by individual incidents of intimidation which continue to be carried out by Kalenjins in the area. In mid-1993, two Luo women were raped by Kalenjins. One was the wife of a school teacher and the other was a sixteen-year-old student who was taken from her house at night and raped in a field.[200] The local police and security officials in the area have not taken any steps to offer greater protection or security to the farm's inhabitants. As long as there is fear that the violence could break out yet again, communities all over the Rift Valley Province will not be able to resettle permanently.

---

[198] Republic of Kenya, *Report of the Parliamentary Select Committee to investigate Ethnic Clashes in Western and Other Parts of Kenya*, p. 45.

[199] Interview with Luo clash victim, Owiro farm, Nandi District, July 2, 1993.

[200] Interview with Luo clash victim, Owiro farm, Nandi District, July 2, 1993.

FOOD SHORTAGE

> *When we feed those who are hungry, we must*
> *also ask why they are hungry.*
> -- NCCK report, The Cursed Arrow

The Rift Valley is the breadbasket of Kenya, yet large areas of Kenya's most fertile land remain uncultivated. Thousands of farmers have not planted, some for two years. Africa Watch visited the Olenguruone area in Nakuru District, where large tracts of land are completely deserted and the houses abandoned by the residents who are too scared to return. The situation is equally bad in other areas of Rift Valley Province.

As a result, the Kenyan government has begun to predict a serious food shortage by the end of 1993. Food dependency is expected to rise dramatically since thousands of previously self-sufficient farmers have lost all their belongings, including their land, and have become completely dependent on food relief. Maize production for 1992 was estimated at 2.34 million tons, a 6.1 percent increase from the previous year, but still 390,000 tons below average. Wheat output fell from 195,000 to 125,000 tons from 1991 to 1992.[201] A Food and Agriculture Organization (FAO) report released in 1993 noted that the victims displaced by the clashes in Rift Valley Province would need 7,200 tons of cereal and 1,080 tons of pulses and other food items in emergency aid in 1993.[202] In the Molo area, the milk supply has dropped from 75,000 liters a month to 29,000.[203]

In anticipation of impending famine, the Kenyan government has appealed to the international community for food aid. In May 1993, President Moi announced that Kenya needed food relief of approximately 176,000 tons in cereals and pulses, and US $31.6 million to transport the food to Northern Kenya and the Rift Valley Province. A church official told Africa Watch bitterly, "food is being burned with the consent of the

---

[201] *Reuters*, June 9, 1993.

[202] "Priority Issue is Food Security," *Daily Nation*, May 14, 1993, p. 6 and "The Real Causes of the Food Deficit," *Daily Nation*, May 23, 1993.

[203] "Nakuru DC Chairs Meeting on Clashes," *Daily Nation*, June 19, 1993.

government, and then they come back and ask the international community for the same."[204]

Since the clash victims are Kenyan citizens in Kenya, they are not considered refugees for the purpose of relief assistance from the United Nations High Commissioner on Refugees (UNHCR). Instead, the Kenyan government has begun negotiations with UNDP to receive assistance from the UN for Kenya's internally displaced.

In May 1993, a UN Disaster Management Team visited Rift Valley Province.[205] The UN team noted in their report that the displaced population had been living in

> appalling conditions for up to one a half years, with irregular supplies of food; no adequate shelter; no access to schooling for the children and only occasional access to basic health facilities . . . people who had trusted in the Government's assurances that security had been re-established had returned home to face sudden death at the hands of their former neighbors.[206]

The team also concluded that there was need for UNDP to play a positive role in addressing this "ongoing national emergency" by sending technical teams to develop strategies and programs. However, the report rightly cautioned that such efforts had to be accompanied by a government commitment at the highest levels to create the conditions conducive to reconciliation, reintegration and enhanced security.[207]

Many Kenyans involved in relief distribution at the moment have strong reservations about UNDP's proposed involvement in food

---

[204] Interview with Rev. Johnson Muhia, Moderator, Elburgon PCEA, Londiani, Kericho District, June 24, 1993.

[205] The delegation consisted of David Whaley, UNDP; Vincent O'Reilly, UNICEF; Else Larsen, WFP; Steve Oti, WHO; G. Guebre-Christos, UNHCR; Don Ferguson, UNDP; and Robert Palmer, UNDP.

[206] UN Disaster Management Team, *Mission to the Affected Areas of Western Kenya affected by the Ethnic Clashes*, May 1993, p. 1-2.

[207] Ibid.

distribution in the clash areas. There is so much distrust among clash victims of the government authorities that local relief workers worry that a food distribution or assistance scheme that is seen to be undertaken with government cooperation will be rejected by the victims. There are also concerns that the government might distribute the relief selectively.

More importantly, there are valid concerns that UNDP involvement will allow government officials to portray the situation as a mere "development problem," and allow them to underplay their damaging political role in fomenting and exacerbating the violence. "If they are not careful, UNDP will depoliticize an issue which is highly politicized," a church official told Africa Watch, "and this will give the government an out in terms of having to deal with it."[208] UNDP must ensure that they cooperate and consult at all steps of the process with the major local donors; the NCCK, the Catholic church and the Kenyan Red Cross.

DEEPENING ETHNIC HATREDS

Inaction and hostility by the government towards the victims of the violence is leading to a growing sentiment that the only option available is for people to arm and defend themselves instead of waiting to be killed. In most places where clashes have taken place, residents continue to fear repeated attacks. One opposition MP told Africa Watch, "it is not surprising to hear that people are beginning to prepare to defend themselves. When they report an incident to the police and nothing is done, what else can they do?"[209]

There have been repeated calls from various groups taking the law into their hands for the formation of private "armies." In June 1993, FORD-A announced that it was going to recruit 10,000 youth wingers for the party who would "help" the government keep peace in Nakuru District. The FORD-A announcement was in response to complaints by Kikuyus in that area that they were being harassed while government forces looked on.[210]

---

[208] Interview with church official, Nairobi, June 21, 1993.

[209] Interview with Martha Karua, DP MP, Nairobi, June 20, 1993.

[210] "Stop This Plans [sic] of Private Armies," *Daily Nation*, June 7, 1993.

In particular, disturbing reports of oathing have been circulating in the country. Oathing is an integral part of the history of resistance in Kenya. During the Mau Mau struggle for independence, fighters swore oaths that bound them to fight British colonial rule to their death.[211] Ordinary citizens that provided food and shelter to the Mau Mau fighters also took these oaths, and the effect was that the British colonial government was never able to infiltrate the Mau Mau movement. Anyone who betrays such an oath, which is performed in complete secrecy, is killed.[212]

Currently, there are reports of oathing being performed on both sides. It is said that many of the Kalenjin warriors that have been attacking took oaths (*muma*) last year with the purpose of driving away all non-Kalenjins from the Rift Valley. There are strong sentiments on the part of the Kalenjin community, supported by government statements, that the multiparty debate is an anti-Kalenjin movement designed to oust their community from power. Any criticism of high-ranking Kalenjin politicians is accordingly viewed as an attack on the community that must be resisted. Kalenjins feel aggrieved by the perception that the other major ethnic groups despise them. Numerous times, Kalenjin clash victims told Africa Watch that the violence began because the Kalenjins were "not respected" or because they were looked down upon. One Kalenjin said "all we want is peace. But peace comes through respect." There is also a strong belief on the part of the Kalenjin warriors that they are carrying out a just demand for "their" land, as the Kikuyu did during the Mau Mau period. An old Kalenjin (Sabaot) man told Africa Watch, "at independence [former President Jomo] Kenyatta gave all the land to the Kikuyus and the Kalenjins got nothing, so now the Kalenjins must take land back."[213]

There have been accounts of oathing being conducted among the Kikuyu community to defend themselves against the Kalenjin attackers and to ensure that Kikuyus do not allow their land to be taken from them

---

[211] Tabitha Kanogo, *Squatters and the Roots of Mau Mau, 1905-63*, Heinemann Kenya Ltd. (1987), p. 133.

[212] NEMU, *Courting Disaster*, April 29, 1993, p. 18.

[213] Interview with old Kalenjin (Sabaot) man, Quintin farm, Trans Nzoia District, June 30, 1993.

in Rift Valley Province. It is also rumored that the oath allows its adherents to retaliate against fellow Kikuyus who leave or sell their land in the Rift Valley Province. At the moment, the oathing in the Kikuyu community seems to be defensive and does not instigate any violence against the Kalenjin community--but as the clashes continue, this could change. On September 5, 1993, Kikuyu MP for Nyeri, Isaiah Mathenge, told the government "not to underestimate the capability of Kenyans to fight injustice since the same people fought the well armed colonialist and won *uhuru* [independence in Kiswahili] using pangas, spears and other home-made weapons."[214]

If the government does not take action to stop the violence and provide a political solution for reconciliation and resettlement, Kenya could slide into civil war. There is increasing determination on the part of both these ethnic groups that they are justified in responding to what they perceive as attacks on their communities. However, there can be no winner in this violence. Although the Kalenjin community has the benefit of state power behind them at the moment, the Kikuyu community is larger and believes that it can outlast the Moi government. Unfortunately, the hatred and ethnic polarization generated by the violence is increasing the prospect of escalating violence and the likelihood of reprisals against the Kalenjin community, if not now, then later.

---

[214] "FORD-K Will Not 'Shift its Mission,'" *Daily Nation*, September 6, 1993.

9. CONCLUSIONS

o   Since the advent of a multiparty system in 1991, following concerted domestic and international pressure, violent fighting between ethnic groups has erupted predominantly in Kenya's most fertile area, the Rift Valley Province. These so-called ethnic clashes are always between the Kalenjin (President Moi's ethnic group) and other ethnic groups.

o   The conflict has been deliberately manipulated and instigated by President Moi and his inner circle and has undermined attempts to create an atmosphere conducive to political pluralism in a multi-party Kenya. Although the violence has been portrayed as the inevitable result of multipartyism in an ethnically diverse country, its immediate causes are political rather than ethnic.

o   The fighting has been continuing on regular basis since October 1991.

o   The violence has resulted in the deaths of over 1,500 people and the displacement of over 300,000. The majority of the victims are non-Kalenjins.

o   The provocation for much of the fighting is attributed to the Kalenjin. Reports of the attacks by these Kalenjin "warriors" are similar. Hundreds of young men, often dressed identically, with traditional bows and arrows attack farms made up predominantly of the Kikuyu, Luo, and Luhya ethnic groups. The attacks are organized and systematic.

o   To a lesser extent, Kalenjins have also been victims of the violence. There have been retaliatory attacks against Kalenjins, although the government has been quicker to provide security in such cases and the violence against the Kalenjins has been more random and opportunistic.

o   The motive for the violence appears multifold: first, to prove the
        government's assertion that multi-party politics would lead to
        tribal chaos. Second, to punish ethnic groups that are perceived
        to support the political opposition, namely the Kikuyu, Luhya
        and Luo. Third, to terrorize and intimidate non-Kalenjins to
        leave the Rift Valley Province, Kenya's most fertile farmland, and
        to allow Kalenjins to take over the land through intimidation and
        violence. Finally, the violence plays a part in renewed calls by
        Kalenjin and Maasai politicians for the introduction of
        majimboism-- a federal system based on ethnicity--which would
        mandate that only members of these minority groups would have
        political and economic power in the Rift Valley Province, which
        has the largest number of Parliamentary seats and is the base of
        Kenya's agricultural economy.

o   The government response to the violence has been characterized
        by inaction toward the attackers and outright hostility against
        others who seek to help the victims. The government declared
        security operation zones in some areas. However, it has yet to
        put an end to the clashes and to resettle the displaced.

o   Kenyan police and security forces have done little to protect the
        victims of the violence.

o   The government has failed in its responsibility to punish those
        responsible for the violence. Most prosecutions have not been
        pursued forcefully and most of those charged, even with the most
        serious offenses, are out on bail. While there have been some
        convictions of Kalenjin attackers, a disproportionate number of
        the convictions have been of non-Kalenjins for possession of
        illegal weapons.

o   Only perhaps a tenth of the Kshs. 10 million [US $125,000] the
        government supposedly pledged for purposes of relief for clash
        victims has been distributed. However, in the few places where
        the government has distributed relief, Africa Watch found that
        Kalenjins and non-Kalenjins had been recipients.

o   The relief and reconciliation efforts of the Kenyan clergy have significantly mitigated the damaging effects of the violence. Most clash victims rely completely on the National Council of Churches of Kenya (NCCK), the Catholic church, the Kenyan Red Cross and a number of smaller relief organizations, for relief assistance in the form of food, shelter, and school fees. In all areas that Africa Watch visited, Kalenjin and non-Kalenjin victims were being assisted equally by the churches.

o   Local government authorities often deny that problems exist, and disperse camps of displaced persons, sometimes forcibly, without regard for their safety in returning to their homes.

o   Many displaced victims are being offered sums significantly lower than market value for their farms. Desperate and destitute, many have sold their land at throwaway prices or swapped it with Kalenjins from other provinces. The pattern of land ownership in Rift Valley Province is being permanently altered as non-Kalenjins sell their land. This has significant political implications because Rift Valley Province has the largest number of Parliamentary seats.

o   The overwhelming majority of the victims are children. Many are traumatized by the violence they have witnessed and most have had their schooling disrupted or terminated. The government consistently closes down makeshift schools that teachers and volunteers attempt to start in the camps for the displaced.

o   An impending food shortage is facing Kenya because large areas in the Rift Valley Province have not been cultivated as a result of the violence.

o   The "security operation zones" declared on September 2, 1993,
         appear to be unconstitutional since October 1, 1993, because
         there has been no Parliamentary resolution approving the order
         within twenty-eight days after it was announced as required by
         the Constitution. The government has used the zones to restrict
         reporting of the clashes by journalists, relief workers, clergy, and
         human rights monitors.

o   The declaration of security operation zones has not put an end
         to the violence, nor has it helped to resettle the displaced.

o   Although ethnic differences and tensions have always existed in
         Kenya, the level of ethnic hatred and destruction caused by the
         recent clashes is previously unknown to Kenya.

o   The ultimate responsibility for ending the violence lies with
         President Moi. Opinion in non-governmental circles in Kenya is
         unanimous: The government could stop the violence if only it
         had the political will, by prosecuting those who are responsible
         for violent acts, investigating and bringing charges where
         appropriate against government officials alleged to be involved
         in instigating attacks, and by providing additional and adequate
         security to areas affected by the violence.

o   If the government does not take steps immediately, the escalating
         violence threatens to spiral into a civil war, for which the
         government will bear a great measure of responsibility.

10. RECOMMENDATIONS

Africa Watch makes the following recommendations to the Kenyan government:

1. The government must take immediate steps to end the violence and to resettle the displaced.

2. The Kiliku Report, prepared by a parliamentary committee, should be adopted and its recommendations implemented by the government. In particular, all allegations of the involvement of government officials in the violence should be investigated and charges brought where there is evidence of wrongdoing.

3. A new Parliamentary Select Committee should be formed to document the violence that has taken place since the release of the Kiliku Report (September 1992) and to reevaluate and update recommendations to the government.

4. Continuing and past attacks should be thoroughly investigated and charges brought where there is evidence against individuals alleged to be responsible.

5. The government must end its discriminatory application of the law. The selective prosecution of government critics must end and action should be taken against government officials and others responsible for inciting violence.

6. Additional and adequate security should be provided for as long as it takes to enable displaced families to return permanently to their land.

7.   Local government officials must stop harassing clash victims by
        forcibly dispersing them from camps where they have
        congregated, and should stop closing down makeshift schools that
        teachers and volunteers in the camps start for the displaced
        children. The government must make efforts to ensure that the
        local government officials in each Province--the PC, DCs, DOs
        and Chiefs--are unbiased and effective in their response to the
        clashes. For example, the system of appointment of local officials
        could be changed to made them elected representatives of the
        local population rather than presidential appointees.

8.   In light of the government's responsibility for spreading the
        violence, the Attorney-General's Office should set up an
        independent commission to inquire into the persistent reports of
        land sales being effected under duress. In cases where displaced
        victims have sold their land at below market prices because of the
        violence, the government should create a process though which
        such land transfers can be reviewed, and, if need be, reversed.
        This commission should also assist victims displaced as a result of
        the violence, where appropriate by payment of compensation to
        those who have lost their land.

9.   A Clash Victims Fund should be created by the government to
        provide compensation and relief assistance to victims and to assist
        in the rebuilding of homes and schools as well as the resumption
        of planting and cultivation.

10.   The government must end the harassment and obstruction of
        humanitarian and relief organizations attempting to assist in the
        relief, reconciliation, and resettlement process.

11.   Police sent to an area to stop the violence must work closely with
        community representatives from all ethnic groups in the area.

12.   The government must permit free movement in the "security
        operation zones," with security escorts if necessary, to all duly
        accredited press correspondents, church relief officials, and
        human rights groups.

Africa Watch makes the following recommendations to the Kenyan political opposition:

1.   The political opposition should stop polarizing the political debate on ethnic lines. Inflammatory statements based on ethnicity should be avoided and reconciliation promoted. The Kalenjin group as a whole should not be indiscriminately held responsible for the actions of the government.

2.   The ethnic clashes should be treated as an issue of national importance by the opposition. Opposition Parliamentarians should introduce a motion each session calling for the recommendations of the Kiliku Report to be adopted by the government and for another Parliamentary Select Committee to update the Kiliku Report.

3.   Cross-party coalitions should be formed to promote relief, reconciliation and resettlement efforts in the clash areas.

Africa Watch makes the following recommendations to the Kenyan non-governmental relief organizations:

1.   Efforts to provide relief and to encourage reconciliation and resettlement should be continued.

2.   A comprehensive and coordinated registration system of the dead and displaced population should be put into place by the various relief organizations. These figures should be updated regularly.

3.   Relief organizations should put into place a mechanism to document and record clashes as they occur and to accompany displaced persons to the police to file a report following an incident.

Africa Watch makes the following recommendations to the donor nations and international relief organizations:

1. Non-development aid to Kenya that is currently suspended should continue to be withheld until there is clear and convincing evidence that the government has taken effective steps to curb the "ethnic" violence and to resettle the displaced. These steps should include, at a minimum, the full and public investigation of allegations of the involvement of government officials in the violence, and the bringing of charges where there is evidence of wrongdoing; the speedy prosecution of all individuals responsible for violent acts; and the provision of additional and adequate security in areas affected by the violence.

2. Foreign governments should publicly raise human rights concerns with the Kenyan government, specifically the evidence of government complicity in the ongoing violence, and call for the government to act to address those concerns.

3. Governments and international relief organizations giving aid to Kenya should consult and cooperate with the local non-governmental community in distributing relief to the clash victims outside government channels.